Media History

Theories, Methods, Analysis

Media History

Theories, Methods, Analysis

edited by

Niels Brügger & Søren Kolstrup

AARHUS UNIVERSITY PRESS

Media History. Theories, Methods, Analysis

Cover photographs: © Erik Holmbjerg/
Scanpix, Nordfoto and Tony Stone Images
Cover design: Jørgen Sparre
Printed in Denmark by Narayana Press, Gylling
ISBN 87 7288 839 3

AARHUS UNIVERSITY PRESS
Langelandsgade 177
8200 Aarhus N
Denmark
Fax (+45) 8942 5380

73 Lime Walk
Headington, Oxford OX3 7AD
United Kingdom
Fax (+44) 1865 750 079

Box 511
Oakville, Conn. 06779
USA
Fax (+ 1) 860 945 9468

www.unipress.dk

Published with support from the Danish Council for the Humanities, Aarhus University Research Foundation and the Department of Information and Media Studies, University of Aarhus.

Table of Contents

Preface

Niels Brügger & Søren Kolstrup

Media history

In the 1970s historical scholarship played a relatively important role within media studies in Denmark. But as Danish media studies expanded in the 1980s and 1990s this role diminished. In this period research focused on new areas of study, especially television, and on new methodologies, especially reception analysis. At the same time media studies engaged more directly in debates about media policy and media politics.

Historical scholarship became, to a certain extent, the neglected child of media studies - in spite of such important exceptions as the history of media reception, and the three-volume history of the Danish media (*Dansk mediehistorie*, 1996-97). The latter project answered a demand for a comprehensive historical survey of Danish media, but it also clearly signaled a need for further and more detailed research within the historical field.

Bearing this context in mind, the time seems right for a general discussion of media history: a discussion that is not only relevant in a Danish perspective, but also relevant to anyone who writes media history. So, although the point of departure is a Danish context, the general discussion of media history is also an international discussion, shedding light on the differences between various national traditions.

In this perspective the Department of Information and Media Studies at the University of Aarhus organised a seminar with the title 'Media History: Theories, Methods, Analysis' (May 16-17 1999). The seminar provided the occasion for reflection on the theoretical and the methodological problems involved in the writing of media histories, and focused attention on already-published histories providing models of empirical research within different media (print media, radio, television). We were happy to receive researchers from America, from the Netherlands as well as from the Nordic countries, and the following seven articles are written with this seminar as their point of departure.

The questions

The articles in this book raise and discuss a number of general issues:

–The definition of 'media',
–The understanding of history,
–The direction of the historic changes, their speed and their perspective,
–The periodisation,
–The source problem.

The definition of 'media'

The definition of 'media' is one of the fundamental issues raised by Niels Brügger in his article 'Theoretical reflections on Media and Media History.' Having asked the question 'What do we actually understand by media?' he presents a theoretical framework for the understanding of relations between the different media and the changing of these relations.

Carin Åberg's approach in 'When the "Wireless" Became Radio' is more empirical. Her point of departure is Patrice Flichy's theories about new technologies and the ways they are used. In fact, a new technology is often used in a manner far removed from the original intention: 'The ideas forming radio as a mass medium can hardly be found in wireless technology, but in the social, cultural and legal implementation of it'. What makes this particular technical device and its (social) use a medium? When does a technical device become a medium?

Another perspective on the definition of media is the question of media as our analytical object. Brügger raises this question by asking how we turn the artifacts called 'media' into objects for study. Søren Kolstrup's article 'The Change of News Structure: Danish Newspapers 1873-1914' is an illustration of the importance of defining the analytical object (in his case a genre): What is news? How can it be defined? How can the artifact 'news story' be turned into an analytical object?

The understanding of history

What are the driving forces or organising principles of media history? What are the roles of social needs or technological changes? How do we understand the conditions, the events and the processes of the past? And how do we turn this into history? These are some of the fundamental questions concerning the understanding of (media) history.

Christopher Anderson and Michael Curtin (in 'Writing Cultural History: The Challenge of Radio and Television') point out that in fact our understanding must take to metaphors or metonymies that in many cases are the only way to understand or describe social processes and changes. The whole process of media changes is understood as a creative destruction illustrated by the Marxian metaphorical description of the industrial epoch: 'all that is solid melts into air.' This grandiose metaphorical understanding is in fact not far from Carin Åberg's more commonsense understanding of media evolution as a social phenomenon related to the totality of social changes.

Sonja de Leeuw's article, 'National Identity and the Dutch Monarchy in Historical Fiction: Revisioning "The Family on the Throne"', treats the relationship between media representations and (the changes of) national identity. She writes: 'Representation is one of the crucial aspects of the relationship between media and society: In what way, by whom and in which context are certain meanings provided by and given to images?' It is argued that the historical evolution is driven by a dialectical movement: On the one hand the article treats upcoming ritual and social events that corroborate national feeling, and on the other hand it treats the transformations within the national ideology as it is constructed in historical television programmes. There is thus a circular movement or a double determination in the evolution of the national feeling in its mediated appearance.

The direction of the historic changes, their speed and their perspective

Does our history have a direction leading from point A to point Z? The question of the direction of history is an issue that is addressed in several articles. Brügger puts the question on the agenda in this way: 'When we turn the past into history, do we then give our history a direction?'

The direction of history is not explicitly discussed in Kolstrup's article, but the historical evolution goes in this article from point A to point Z. The news story is characterised by one structure in the initial phase and by a different structure in the final phase, both points being well defined. The intermediate points B to Y, are vague and seem from the very beginning to tend against Z.

Åberg sees the changes of the radio genres not as a single movement with an initial state and a final state, but more as an experimentarium where new parallel form(at)s are constantly tried out and where final states and initial states cannot really be distinguished. The elaboration of these two new genres is not seen as a single linear development from A to B, but more as a steadily ongoing process where different new formats are tried out at the same time and eventually abandoned.

Not only the direction but also the speed and the perspective of the historical changes are discussed. Kolstrup's point of departure is the distinction elaborated by the French *Annales School* of history between long-term, medium-term and short-term developments. In short-term history we could include the history of events, and often the history of institutions also, as manifested in rapid changes in a particular organisation. Medium-term history could be illustrated by the transformation of genres, of media (if the media is not seen as a superficial phenomenon) and of institutions, especially if the transformation of institutions is seen as a cultural phenomenon in several organisations at the same time. And as for the transformations within long-term history they are rarely conscious to the social actors, e.g. reading habits, the beliefs of the public or the tastes of the public: Which stories remain popular even when they change genre?

Anderson and Curtin describe the classical media history as a history that concentrates on institutions and artifacts: technological innovations and competition between actors/institutions. This is the history of the great innovators, history written as a top-down construction (history seen from the point-of-view of the prominent leaders and institutions) and in the French *Annales School*'s understanding it is a short-term history. The long-term history corresponds in many respects to history written from below. The media are seen as the products of collective social engagement, they are seen as 'constructed complexes of habits, beliefs, and procedures imbedded in elaborate codes of communication, the history is never more than the history of their uses...' This is the bottom-up perspective 'the fabric of everyday life.'

Gunhild Agger (in 'Proximity and Distance: Perspectives for Analysis of TV Fiction and its History') does not directly mention the temporal modes, nor does she use the spatial metaphors in her description. But she uses the opposition proximity/distance as a fundamental dichotomy. It is her thesis that proximity and distance have been organising principles in mass communication since the establishment of the printing press. The very existence of this opposition since the beginning of mass communication means that we are dealing with the long-term history.

Åberg prefers to see the evolution in a bottom-up perspective, and so does Per Jauert (in 'Reflections on Writing Radio History: an Essay') who sees mainly the changes of radio from inside or bottom-up and he is close to Anderson and Curtin when he points out the three central issues: a) What is the nature of radio? b) How have those qualities been framed institutionally as a structure? And finally, c) the cultural issue: How did the audience perceive and use radio? What was the impact of radio on everyday life?

Most of the articles are thus a perfect example that some way or another media history has changed the perspective from short-term history to some kind of long-term history. Culture and not events are in focus.

The periodisation

'Should our history be divided into different slices of time?', Brügger asks. This question implies two further questions: The question of the length of the 'slices', and the question of how distinctive the ruptures between the slices are.

The problem of periodisation is fundamental in Aggers article. What are the criteria for periodisation? How can we define short periods? And especially how can we define a period that has hardly yet come to its end: 1988-97? Agger points out that it is easier to define short periods if we stay inside the local or the national framework, whereas the problems of periodisation increase when we are at a transnational level. Agger also demonstrates that we get different periodisations according to the prevailing features chosen: In television history we get one periodisation if we use the programming as criterion and another if we choose institutional features. As for the period 1988-97, in Danish media history it could be founded on two salient traits: Belonging (cultural/national) and breakdown of the traditional political boundaries as they are thematised on television.

The notion of rupture becomes less crucial in this context. In fact, the notion of rupture is very handy if you apply the short-term perspective to the institutional history. Changing the Danish newspaper *Politiken* in 1905 might be seen as a total rupture with the past due to the influence and the professional insight of the director of this newspaper (Cavling): The Cavling perspective. But Kolstrup argues that if the entire changing of newspaper reading and production around the turn of the century is taken into consideration, this apparent rupture is diluted into a huge number of different transformations, each being of greater or lesser importance and degrees of rapidity.

The source problem

Finally some articles treat the source problem, the weight to be given to empirical data and/or to interpretation of different other sources. These problems are, of course, crucial to any historical description or presentation, but in this volume they are most directly addressed by Jauert who points out and treats two issues: a) The empirical reference to specific sources/data and, b) The reference to more general data/descriptions and interpretations. In the first case the sources yield direct information, in the second case the historian combines different historical disciplines and factual information in order to shed light on a new historical event or state.

The articles

Although the following articles, seen as a whole, do treat media history from a theoretical, a methodological and an analytical perspective, the weight of these three themes is not the same in each of the texts: they either have a theoretical, a methodological or an analytical bias. In order to reflect these differences of weight we have arranged the articles in such a way that anybody reading the book from one end to the other will experience an overall movement from the theoretical towards the analytical.

But this is not the only principle of arrangement. The order of the articles also reflects the history of the emergence of the media on which they focus. Thus, anybody who reads the book from one end to the other will also experience a movement throughout the history of media, from the printing press to radio, and ending with television.

Of course, the coexistence of these two principles cannot be carried through completely, for instance the first article does indeed have a theoretical bias, but it also deals with both radio and television. Nevertheless it is our hope, that the reader will forgive us for not being able to align the articles according to one strictly logical principle.

Thanks

We would like to thank the following for making the publication of this book possible: The Department of Information and Media Studies at the University of Aarhus for organising the seminar on 'Media History' and for their kind financial support to this book; the Aarhus University Research Foundation as well as the Danish Council for the Humanities for their generous financial contribution; the contributing authors for their enthusiasm and diligence; and finally the publisher, Aarhus University Press, for assistance and patience throughout the project.

Niels Brügger & Søren Kolstrup
Aarhus, February 2002

Writing Cultural History

The Challenge of Radio and Television

Christopher Anderson & Michael Curtin

The radio and television signals that endlessly circle the globe, scattered by antennae, bounced off satellites, or streaming through wires, are invisible to the naked eye and silent to the ear alone. Carried along by waves that break unseen against distant shores, these signals trace the ebb and flow of modern life; they are both a foundation for modern societies and a restless current of change running through them. However invisible or evanescent they may be, radio and television signals form the bridge between public and private life in modern societies. These signals - weightless yet dense, ephemeral yet enduring - are an embodiment of modernity, an expression of the contradictions inherent in the historical period that began with the consolidation of industrial capitalism in the nineteenth century. This should come as no surprise; the large-scale integration of financial and industrial centres with distant markets and remote sources of raw material was fully realised only after the introduction of electric communication, in the form of the telegraph, removed the obstacle of distance. By transforming the experience of space and time, electric communication lies at the very heart of the historical processes of modernity.[1]

1. This idea is elaborated most effectively in the work of Harold Innis. See *Empire and Communication* (Innis 1950) and *The Bias of Communication* (Innis 1951). James Carey provides both commentary on Innis and his own influential studies in *Communication as Culture* (Carey 1989). In describing the social processes of modernity, many scholars outside the field of communication have acknowledged the crucial role of electronic media in the transformation of time and space. See, for instance, Anthony Giddens *The Consequences of Modernity* (Giddens 1990), Stephen Kern *The Culture of Time and Space, 1880-1918* (Kern 1983), Roger Friedland and Dierdre Boden (eds.) *NowHere: Space, Time and Modernity* (Friedland & Boden →

Since the nineteenth century, artists and intellectuals have tried to explain the permanent revolution that jolts modern societies like an endless electrical current. In the profoundly material world of the industrial age – a world of monolithic factories and clamorous machines, roaring locomotives, soaring skyscrapers, resplendent department stores stocked with brilliantly packaged goods – the foundations of social life became less tangible with the passing of time; instead of crumbling beneath the pressure and pace of the modern era, they seemed to evaporate before one's eyes. In one of the great modern poems, Yeats admonished his readers to behold these conditions: 'Things fall apart; the centre cannot hold. Mere anarchy is loosed upon the world.' Marx and Engels saw the social pressures associated with capitalism – 'constant revolutionising of production, uninterrupted disturbance of all social conditions, everlasting uncertainty and agitation' – as the driving force of modernity. 'All that is solid melts into air', they announced in a phrase famous for identifying the 'creative destruction' of modernity. By describing a convergence of substance and action in which a recognisable social reality evaporates, yet is still experienced as a material presence, this phrase also anticipated the paradox of electronic communication, which has a tangible presence despite its elusive physical form. As social life plays out amidst the restless energy of electronic signals, even the most formidable monuments of history, tradition, authority, and belief melt into air, carried away in the vapour trail of radio and television transmissions.[2]

→ 1994). There are many useful discussions of modernity as an historical period. A useful volume is Stuart Hall, David Held, Don Hubert, and Kenneth Thompson *Modernity* (Hall, Held, Hubert & Thompson 1996).

2. The Yeats quotation is from his poem, 'The Second Coming.' The quotation from Marx and Engels appears in *The Communist Manifesto*. Paul Berman first drew attention to this phrase of Marx and Engels as a metaphor for the experience of modernity, although he does not discuss the electronic media, in *All That is Solid Melts Into Air* (Berman 1982). For specific discussion of the media and modernity, see Paddy Scannell *Radio, Television and Modern Life* (Scannell 1996) and John B. Thompson *The Media and Modernity* (Thompson 1995), Graham Murdock 'Communications and the constitution of modernity' (Murdock 1993).

Marx and Engels turned to metaphor to describe these social processes because metaphor alone offered a way to express the contradictions of modernity. Media are often treated as rock-solid facts, but they too are really only comprehensible to us through the figurative language of metaphor and metonymy. In spite of their complexity as social and technical achievements, communications media are identified either through metonymy, as when a medium is defined solely by its technology (radio, television), or metaphorically, in terms used to describe their operation (broadcast, transmit), institutional structure (chain, network, World Wide Web), or the social relations they support (audience, nation, virtual community). In part each of these terms carries meanings that influence and eventually constrain our ability to think about electronic communication, because we forget that the terms are (or once were) figurative and begin to perceive them as irreducible facts. Of course, at some fundamental level all human cognition and communication relies on metaphor, but it is still worth considering how thoroughly we conceive of electronic communication in figurative terms and how difficult it would be to do otherwise.

The recognition that communications media such as radio and television are apprehended metaphorically sets the stage for the cultural turn in American media history over the past fifteen years. This shift in perspective recognises that media are not the given facts that precede historical investigation or the bedrock upon which any historical investigation takes place; they are ongoing social productions, defined and redefined through use, affected not only by events and material conditions, but, crucially, by the language used to describe and discuss them.[3] Traditional histories of electronic media concentrated on institutions and artifacts: technological innovation, competition among electronics manufacturers, the rise of networks and the development of advertising, the politics of federal policy-making and regulation. This was history written 'from above', which assumed that radio and television were created by the actions of great men,

3. See the work of Carey mentioned above, Daniel Czitrom *Media and the American Mind* (Czitrom 1983), John Durham Peters *Speaking into the Air* (Peters 1999), Jeffrey Sconce *Haunted Media* (Sconce 2000).

powerful corporations, and the Federal government. It offered a meaningful framework for understanding the media, one in which individual media are treated as objects, easily identifiable and distinguishable from other media and from other social practices and institutions.[4]

More recent histories, those written 'from below', have begun to view the media as the products of a collective social engagement, a struggle for definition involving not only powerful institutions but also each of us who uses media technologies or encounters radio and TV programs in our daily lives. Through these ordinary encounters with home electronic equipment, broadcast programming schedules, or the stories, images, and arguments made available on our radio and TV receivers, we continuously construct and reconstruct the media. In spite of the terms we use to identify particular media or the technology involved in transmission or reception, one medium is not easily distinguishable from another, and no medium is inert. 'Media are not fixed natural objects', historian Carolyn Marvin has argued, 'they have no natural edges. They are constructed complexes of habits, beliefs, and procedures embedded in elaborate codes of communication. The history of media is never more or less than the history of their uses, which always leads away from them [the media] to the social practices and conflicts they illuminate'.[5] By conceiving of media as contingent historical formations and not as enduring institutions, social and cultural historians have discovered new sites of historical inquiry at every level of society and have even reoriented traditional institutional histories.[6]

4. The most important such history is Erik Barnouw's masterful three-volume *A History of Broadcasting in the United States* (Barnouw 1966-1970).
5. Carolyn Marvin *When Old Technologies Were New* (Marvin 1988, 8).
6. For example, see Lynn Spigel's groundbreaking *Make Room For TV* (Spigel 1992), which reoriented television history by shifting perspective away from media institutions to the struggles involved in the integration of television sets and programs into the postwar American family and the family home. See also Lynn Spigel and Denise Mann, (eds.) *Television and the Female Consumer* (Spigel & Mann 1992).

Whereas broadcast programs were once given short-shift by historians who were more interested in the economics or politics of broadcasting than in its cultural consequences, programs are now seen as truly significant cultural artifacts. The production process no longer needs to be depicted as an assembly line where the beleaguered spirit of creativity runs up against the overwhelming machinery of corporate constraint; instead, archival research suggests that, in order to produce meaningful artifacts, radio and television production involves a series of intricate negotiations within a hierarchy of shifting power relations. The programs emerge from diverse aesthetic traditions, make use of complicated narrative and rhetorical strategies, and express a surprising range of meanings in response to their historical contexts. Moreover, it is no longer assumed that all audience members find a uniform meaning or pleasure in these programs. Media historians now choose to account for the production and reception of broadcast programming, not as a dollop of flavour added to a 'more substantial' history of the medium or as a reflection of more decisive historical forces, but as the very fabric of media history.[7]

Similarly, histories of communication technologies no longer depict an inevitable march of scientific and technological progress led by resourceful inventors and titans of industry. Instead, media historians have shifted attention to the social and cultural contexts in which technologies are designed and produced, the expert voices who introduce them to the public, the marketing strategies used to promote them as consumer goods, the regulatory debates and policies that constrain their use, and, most importantly, the ways in which ordinary people integrate these technologies into their lives. Technologies are no longer seen as indifferent conveyers of meaning and experience, but as significant cultural artifacts that require, and reward, close

7. See Robert C. Allen *Speaking of Soap Operas* (Allen 1985), Julie D'Acci *Defining Wome* (D'Acci 1994), Christopher Anderson *Hollywood TV* (Anderson 1994), Michael Curtin *Redeeming the Wasteland* (Curtin 1995), Nina C. Leibman *Living Room Lectures* (Leibman 1995), John Thornton Caldwell *Televisuality* (Caldwell 1995), Michele Hilmes *Radio Voices* (Hilmes 1997), Lynn Spigel and Michael Curtin (eds.) *The Revolution Wasn't Televised* (Spigel & Curtin 1997), Susan Douglas *Listening In* (Douglas 1999).

scrutiny by those who seek to understand the media in historical terms.[8]

This, then, is the major shift in perspective among historians of radio and television – from a concern with the institutional forms of broadcasting to the social and cultural contexts within which people encounter and use the media, and from the dismissal of media content as the colourful byproduct of media institutions to a recognition that radio and television programs are richly meaningful cultural artifacts. Still, the question remains: Why has the history of radio and television taken a cultural turn during the past fifteen years? A search for the answer points toward two historical developments. First, media historians have been influenced by both the turn to social and cultural analysis in many areas of historical research and the rise of cultural studies within media studies. The cultural studies movement began by reassessing presumptions about the role of popular media in modern life and, therefore, has had a major impact on historians directly concerned with popular media. Second, scholars have responded to historical conditions affecting the broadcast media, particularly the slow eclipse of national-scale broadcasting, which demands explanation from any number of perspectives, including historical inquiry into the origins and expansion of broadcasting as a model for electronic communication. We will discuss both of these developments below.

Historical scholarship

If recent developments among electronic media have encouraged new perspectives on media history, then changes in the theory and practice of historical research have forged new tools for media historians and a new orientation toward the object of study. Social and cultural historians, particularly scholars working from a feminist or Marxist

8. See Susan Douglas *Inventing American Broadcasting, 1899-1922* (Douglas 1987), Michele Hilmes *Hollywood and Broadcastin* (Hilmes 1990), William Boddy *Fifties Television* (Boddy 1990), Susan Smulyan *Selling Radio* (Smulyan 1994), Thomas Streeter *Selling the Air* (Streeter 1996).

orientation, have played a prominent role in these intellectual developments. In part this represents the influence of a general movement in historiography – a shift away from 'top-down' perspectives that concentrate on prominent leaders and the institutions of power toward 'bottom-up' perspectives that examine the fabric of everyday life while seeking out voices neglected or silenced by traditional histories. Labour historians and feminist scholars played a prominent role in shifting attention to the lives of ordinary people, who would ultimately make up the audiences for network broadcasting, and to the relations of power involved in and enacted through historical processes. Such research has fostered attempts to understand the relationships between cultural representation and forms of identity, especially in regard to issues of class, nation, gender, race, and sexual orientation.[9] With its emphasis on the act of reception as the decisive moment in the circulation of meanings, cultural studies also supported the shift of attention from the history of institutions to that of reception and use.

Another benefit of the cultural turn in recent scholarship is that programs are now studied as texts, and not merely as the residue of industrial systems or responses to policy initiatives or the reflection of social concerns. Much previous work attended to these media because they involved enormous corporations, represented powerful economic forces, or exercised social pre-eminence. Research of this sort would account for everything but the programs that drew viewers to the media in the first place. Fortunately, this is no longer true. Programming is now seen to play a crucial role in the processes by which television, for instance, performs its characteristic double mediation – incorporating issues and concerns from society, refracting them through the institutions of television, and transmitting them back to

9. There are many books that discuss the cultural turn in historiography and social analysis. See, for example, Lynn Hunt (ed.) *The New Cultural History* (Hunt 1989), Nicholas B. Dirks, Geoff Eley and Sherry B. Ortner (eds.) *Culture/Power/History* (Dirks, Eley & Ortner 1994), Joyce Appleby, Lynn Hunt and Margaret Jacobs *Telling the Truth About History* (Appleby, Hunt & Jacobs 1994), Victoria E. Bonnell and Lynn Hunt (eds.) *Beyond the Cultural Turn* (Bonnell & Hunt 1999).

society in a recognisable form.[10] Thus, entertainment programming becomes as important as news and current affairs in any effort to understand the social meanings of television.

The cultural history of radio and television benefits also from another theoretical insight of cultural studies, the concept of 'articulation', as discussed by Stuart Hall and others.[11] As a cultural theory, 'articulation' emphasises the connections that may link relatively autonomous social and cultural practices under specific historical conditions. For example, the professional ideologies of television producers may at certain moments 'articulate' with the commercial goals of advertisers to create a program that serves as the ideal environment for advertising. But this outcome is not inevitable. In fact, it is equally possible for a television program – such as the lurid, sexually-obsessed daytime talk shows of the 1990s – to attract huge audiences and still not receive the support of advertisers, many of whom decide that the program fails to provide a 'proper' environment for their products. Rather than resort to a unified theory of power, such as one that views the media industries as agents of social domination, cultural studies focus on the relative autonomy and interdependence of social and cultural practices throughout society. Historical research is essential in this case, because no theory can predict precisely how these practices will be articulated under particular conditions. The historian's goal is to account for the dynamic interplay of forces that together constitute what we refer to simply as 'radio' or 'television' at any given moment: industry, technology, regulation, programming, reception, and use.

Such an approach pays special attention to the complexities and contradictions – the contingent nature – of historical phenomena and therefore relies on the targeted case study instead of the broad historical narrative to account for the unpredictable density of any particu-

10. See John Corner *Critical Ideas in Television Studies* (Corner 1999), John Hartley *Uses of Television* (Hartley 1999).

11. As many have discussed, this use of the term 'articulation' depends upon its dual meaning in Great Britain, where it means both 'speaking an utterance' and also 'making a connection'. The latter usage is not common in American English. See, for instance, David Morley and Kuan-Hsing Chen (eds.) *Stuart Hall* (Morley & Chen 1996).

lar instance, as well as the inescapable limits of any historian's perspective. When television is treated as a shallow and impoverished cultural form, it is relatively easy to write a broad history of the medium. But an historian attuned to the medium's cultural resonance, one who sees television as a rich cultural form, must come to terms with the sheer cultural weight of any particular moment in the endless flow of television. Historians of broadcast media must develop strategies for coping with peculiar surpluses and deficits of historical evidence.

On the one hand, historians are faced with an almost overwhelming surplus of certain types of information and texts. How, for instance, does one avoid being superficial or reductive in writing about a television series' narrative consisting of hundreds of episodes that were produced over years and may have been viewed in many different historical contexts? How can one make sense of the range of programs running simultaneously on competing channels? How does one account for that quality which Charlotte Brunsdon has described as the 'televisionness' of television – the endless, irreducible, ever-multiplying flow of images and sounds that are somehow integrated into the everyday lives of viewers? Since Raymond Williams developed his concept of 'flow', scholars have ceaselessly attempted to come to terms with the peculiar form of television's textual organisation, one which exceeds all familiar boundaries and poses enormous methodological challenges for an historian.[12]

On the other hand, historians also discover severe deficits of information, particularly when studying aspects of television that lie beyond the concern of institutional record-keeping. This includes virtually all knowledge about the historical reception of television, since ordinary viewers do not leave traces of their presence on the historical record. One also discovers a large gap in the historical record before the advent of reliable and affordable recording equipment and, after recording was possible, because recordings of radio and TV broadcasts initially weren't deemed worthy of preservation. Countless hours of live radio and television programming or improperly preserved videotape recordings have been lost forever. In both cases, historians

12. Charlotte Brunsdon 'What is the "Television" of Television Studies?' (Brunsdon 1997), Raymond Williams *Television* (Williams 1974).

must develop strategies for filling these gaps and recovering as much as possible of that which has been lost in the history of electronic media.

The cultural turn in media history encourages a writing of histor*ies* rather than history, the detailed case study rather than the sweeping narrative. For radio and television historians influenced by cultural studies, the goal is not simply to construct an authoritative narrative of the past, but to understand these media as complex social and cultural formations that are produced, reproduced, and revised in an ongoing process. By remaining aware of the interventions required to manage both the surpluses and deficits of available evidence, historians obviously know that their conclusions are at best provisional – and that their conclusions contribute to the ongoing process that provides a recognisable form to the experience of radio and television.

The end of broadcasting

The historical studies of radio and television published since the early to mid-1980s were written during the twilight of broadcasting, a period in which the traditional American broadcast networks and the European public service networks faced several major challenges, most prominently from competition encouraged by new video technologies, such as cable TV and home video, in a climate of sweeping regulatory change. Until the 1970s American television had been virtually synonymous with the three major networks, and one could easily assume that the major networks were the natural and inevitable form of television. We refer to this as the 'network era' in which broadcast radio and television were developed and dominated by monopolistic national networks that transmitted their programming to a massive audience of viewers who watched on receivers in their homes. By the 1960s, the three major networks in the United States (ABC, CBS, NBC) reached more than ninety percent of television households during a typical evening. In European countries, national public service broadcasting was equally dominant during this era of monopolistic broadcasting.

The network era has been in decline since the mid-1980s, as the American broadcast networks, along with many public service networks in Europe, began to face intense competition for viewers in an increasingly commercialised environment. By looking at the network era, beginning with the formation of broadcast networks in radio and moving through the recent challenges to network television, as an historically bounded phenomenon, media historians may shed light on changes currently taking place. We already find ourselves amidst different - perhaps radically different - conditions than those of the network era. Contemporary television is characterised by several features that signal the end of the broadcasting model of electronic communication associated with the national networks: increased channel availability (through cable and satellite distribution), niche networks aimed at highly differentiated audiences, technologies of viewer discretion and interaction (VCR, remote control, 'Web TV'), extended signal range - particularly across national borders - due to satellite transmission, and centreless networks, such as the Internet. The networks' share of the television audience has steadily dwindled over the past two decades, and commercial broadcast networks are no longer assured of an annual profit.

It is now possible to see the network era as a distinct moment in history, a transitory convergence of historical forces that produced a particular contingent response, and not as the natural, inevitable, or permanent form of radio and television in the industrialised world. Network broadcasting organised on a national scale was neither a natural application of radio and television technology, nor an inevitable product of social and economic forces; instead, it was a social and cultural achievement, supported by some social groups and resisted by others, tied to a particular form of modern consumer culture and the modern nation-state. The decline of the network era reminds us that history moves in no particular direction or toward no particular conclusion. Instead, it reveals the uneven development and unstable nature of national network broadcasting. Historians are more than ever aware of ambivalent audience responses to media technology and programming, public debates over use of the electromagnetic spectrum, and internal conflicts within the television industry. Network broadcasting was not an incipient structure awaiting discovery; it has existed tenuously in a climate of ongoing controversy, deliberation, and experimentation.

By recognising that network broadcasting is a contingent, historical phenomenon, our attention begins to shift from the technical achievement of radio and television to an essentially social activity – the development of national communication networks. Such networks are among the definitive traits of modernity: the transmission of images and ideas from a central source to geographical peripheries, making possible the large-scale organisation of society across space and time. Traditional broadcast histories have emphasised the integrative social function of these networks, portraying the airwaves as a public resource governed by the modern nation-state. This function of radio and television networks is most apparent in countries where broadcasting developed as a public service and broadcasts themselves were seen as aiding in the construction of national citizenship. The networks have served a similar function in the U.S., even though the airwaves were given over to commercial interests rather than reserved for government use. This led to a situation, peculiar to American broadcasting, in which networks promoted a form of national citizenship refracted primarily through the lens of consumer culture and, therefore, introduced the characteristic tension at the heart of American broadcasting, the contradiction between the two social identities proffered by radio and television: those of citizen and consumer.

Broadcast networks – whether devoted to the construction of citizens or consumers – not only made national audiences possible by calling attention to the simultaneity of experience in far-flung locales, they also helped to organise popular perceptions of time and space through daily, weekly, and seasonal broadcast schedules, and the distinction between national and local programming. A fundamental social experience of individuals in the modern era involves imagining the distant presence of other citizens tuned into the same broadcast, brought together by a common knowledge of national brand advertising, network schedules, and series programming. National broadcasting helped to create new forms of collective experience, but also etched the lines of social difference in various rites of inclusion and exclusion – from the moral instruction of situation comedies to the 'separate-but-equal' forms of racial representation that continue to provoke protest. National radio and television are not simply devices for social reproduction, but sites for an ongoing struggle between forces of social integration and difference, control and contest.

Just as social and cultural histories of broadcasting ask us to look beyond the institutions and technologies that have populated traditional histories, they also ask us to shift our attention from momentous media events to the banal forms of radio and television experienced in everyday life. Traditional histories have emphasised coverage of key national events that seem to exemplify the civic role of television – the Kennedy funeral, the Vietnam War, the moon landing. Historians now direct attention toward the more quotidian forms of television programming – the continuing series that filled the networks' prime-time evening schedules and the daytime serials and talk shows aimed initially at women – because the routine experience of television is as important as 'event' or current affairs programming in producing a truly national citizenry. More than any other cultural form, prime-time radio and television became the site for producing a popular and collective sense of identity. Indeed, the network era was epitomised by the concept of prime time, those hours in every evening of every week of every year in which the networks attempted to transcend social differences and present stories and images that captivated the largest possible audience. Whether the public accepted, disputed, or even rejected the proffered images of collective national experience, prime-time network broadcasting set the terms of American national identity for much of the twentieth century.

The recent decline in prime-time viewership for the major networks, along with the rise of specialised cable networks and the segmentation of the audience into smaller, demographically-targeted markets, has transformed television in the United States. The prime-time schedules of the three formerly monopolistic networks now attract fewer than half of the nation's television viewers – a far cry from the vast numbers who tuned in during the 1960s and '70s. Even as the prime-time network schedule loses its salience for many Americans, who are as likely to watch professional wrestling on a cable network as to watch a situation comedy on the major networks, the idea of prime time and of traditional broadcast networks still frames the way we talk about television, whether we are discussing the quality of network programming, the effects of media use on children, or the implications of media portrayals on gender politics or race relations. Even in the television industry, according to a recent article in the trade magazine *Variety*, network executives operate 'virtually the same way they did when Lucy and Desi were TV's hot couple'.

As a culture, we continue to act as if prime-time network television is a village green, neighbourhood tavern, intellectual salon, and primal campfire all rolled into one – the site where we regularly gather in order to tell tales and debate issues that renew our collective sense of identity and mission. In this lingering image, prime time is more than a schedule segment. Prime time is an unrecognised ritual that performs a particular vision of social knowledge and cultural authority while attempting to address the largest public imaginable in the modern world. The emergence, development, and ongoing production of prime time is a distinctive achievement in human history, and yet we largely take it for granted, even at a moment when it is rapidly being eclipsed.

The rise and decline of prime time is intertwined with the production of a specific set of social relations that could not have existed without network broadcasting. In particular, the networks fostered the growth of national mass marketing and mass consumption, which in turn facilitated the expansion of monopoly capitalism and factory-based mass production. The network era now appears to have been intimately tied to a particular set of modern historical conditions, including unprecedented economic expansion and corporate growth, the consolidation of the modern nation-state, and the presumed existence of a coherent national public.

Since the 1970s, however, national and regional economies have changed dramatically as a result of globalisation, and this has occurred alongside equally significant transitions in politics, society, and culture. This new era is characterised by widespread industry deregulation, the decline or privatisation of 'public service' institutions, a growing emphasis on niche markets, flexible production practices, and transnational flows of goods, images, and people. Both the nation-state and broadcast networks have come under pressure as the forces of a global cultural economy relentlessly violate the integrity of national boundaries and the logic of national networks. The idea of a national audience that regularly engages a common body of network programs is anachronistic in the emerging media environment, in which audiences can be miniscule and specific, as for a cable channel like Home and Garden Television, or unimaginably large and dispersed, in the case of a global satellite channel like CNN.

The network era – as a model of social organisation, a technical achievement, and the epitome of mass culture – has been an exceptionally powerful historical phenomenon, but it has begun to disappear after less than a century of existence. The cultural histories of radio and television have appeared, because it now seems necessary to ask: What *was* the network era? How did programming of the network era address viewers and attempt to constitute a national audience? How did the networks and advertisers encourage collective identities and, at the same time, mark social difference? How did network radio and television both facilitate and respond to the century's economic, social, and political changes?

Conclusion

Histories of radio and television are oriented toward events in the past, of course, but the emergence of new social and cultural histories over the last fifteen years, particularly as it has coincided with a major redefinition of network broadcasting in the United States and Europe, appears to offer a timely historical context for understanding the new media environment of cable TV, satellites, home video, computers, and the Internet. We may not know what form the electronic media will take in the new century, but it is increasingly clear that we stand on the far side of a divide which separates us from a distinct historical period whose time largely has passed. The attempts to look anew at the history of radio and television have given rise to a diverse body of scholarship that represents a range of orientations – toward the past, toward the project of writing history, toward the phenomena of electronic communication, and toward the responsibilities of an historian.

Still, we need to be aware of the ways in which a long-held image of the network era serves as a conceptual framework that still influences critical thought about television and the more recent technologies of electronic communication. This image of television, which coalesced during the network era and depicts a broadcast medium monopolised by powerful corporate or government interests while being aimed at an indiscriminate mass audience, serves as the convenient metaphor that continues to set the terms for most discussions of the medium (such as the indefatigable media violence debates). Such is the power of this dominant image of television; it survives even though it bears little resemblance to contemporary forms and experiences of television.

An historical awareness of the network era, which views it as a moment in history and not the natural form of television, should enable us to sketch out a framework for understanding television now that the metaphor of broadcasting no longer suffices. We began by asking, 'What was network television?' in order to ask another question: 'What is television in the new century?' With an historical understanding of radio and television, we should be better suited for mapping the terrain of a new form of television that is already upon us: dispersed throughout society and no longer confined to the home, targeted for segmented audiences with specific tastes, global in scale and in outlook, linked to the centreless networks of the Internet and the commodified networks of media conglomerates, familiar enough to recognise instinctively, yet strange enough to be occasionally and unexpectedly exotic. Our goal is not to forecast the future of television, but to provide a more useful framework for understanding what television is becoming.

References

D'Acci, Julie 1994. *Defining Women: The Case of Cagney and Lacey*. Chapel Hill: University of North Carolina Press.

Allen, Robert C. 1985. *Speaking of Soap Operas*. Chapel Hill: University of North Carolina Press.

Anderson, Christopher 1994. *Hollywood TV: The Studio System in the Fifties*. Austin: University of Texas Press.

Appleby, Joyce, Lynn Hunt & Margaret Jacobs 1994. *Telling the Truth About History*. New York: Norton.

Barnouw, Erik 1966-1970. *A History of Broadcasting in the United States*. New York: Oxford University Press.

Berman, Paul 1982. *All That is Solid Melts Into Air: The Experience of Modernity*. New York: Simon and Schuster.

Boddy, William 1990. *Fifties Television: The Industry and Its Critics*. Champaign: University of Illinois Press.

Bonnell Victoria E. & Lynn Hunt (eds.) 1999. *Beyond the Cultural Turn:*

New Directions in the Study of Society and Culture. Berkeley: University of California Press.

Brunsdon, Charlotte 1997. What is the 'Television' of Television Studies?. Christine Geraghty & David Lusted (eds.), *The Television Studies Book*, London: Edwin Arnold.

Caldwell, John Thornton 1995. *Televisuality: Style, Crisis, and Authority in American Television*. New Brunswick: Rutgers University Press.

Carey, James 1989. *Communication as Culture: Essays on Media and Society*. Boston: Unwin Hyman.

Corner, John 1999. *Critical Ideas in Television Studies*. London: Oxford University Press.

Curtin, Michael 1995. *Redeeming the Wasteland: Television Documentary and Cold War Politics*. New Brunswick: Rutgers University Press.

Czitrom, Daniel 1983. *Media and the American Mind: From Morse to McLuhan*. Chapel Hill: University of North Carolina Press.

Dirks, Nicholas B., Geoff Eley & Sherry B. Ortner (eds.) 1994. *Culture/Power/History*. Princeton: Princeton University Press.

Douglas, Susan 1987. *Inventing American Broadcasting, 1899-1922*. Baltimore: Johns Hopkins University Press.

Douglas, Susan 1999. *Listening In: Radio and the American Imagination*. New York: Times Books.

Friedland, Roger Dierdre Boden (eds.) 1994. *NowHere: Space, Time and Modernity*. Berkeley: University of California Press.

Giddens, Anthony 1990. *The Consequences of Modernity*. Stanford: Stanford University Press.

Hall, Stuart, David Held, Don Hubert & Kenneth Thompson 1996. *Modernity: An Introduction to Modern Societies*. London: Blackwell.

Hartley, John 1999. *Uses of Television*. New York: Routledge.

Hilmes, Michele 1990, *Hollywood and Broadcasting: From Radio to Cable*. Champaign: University of Illinois Press.

Hilmes, Michele 1997. *Radio Voices: American Broadcasting, 1922-1952*. Minneapolis: University of Minnesota Press.

Hunt, Lynn (ed.) 1989. *The New Cultural History*. Berkeley: University of California Press.

Innis, Harold 1950. *Empire and Communication*. Oxford: Oxford University Press.

Innis, Harold 1951. *The Bias of Communication*. Toronto: University of Toronto Press.

Kern, Stephen 1983. *The Culture of Time and Space, 1880-1918*. Cambridge: Harvard University Press.

Leibman, Nina C. 1995. *Living Room Lectures: The Fifties Family in Film and Television*. Austin: University of Texas Press.

Marvin, Carolyn 1988. *When Old Technologies Were New: Thinking About Electric Communication in the Late Nineteenth Century*. New York: Oxford University Press.

Morley, David & Kuan-Hsing Chen (eds.) 1996. *Stuart Hall: Critical Dialogues in Cultural Studies*. New York: Routledge.

Murdock, Graham 1993. Communications and the constitution of modernity. *Media, Culture & Society* 15(4), 521-39.

Peters, John Durham 1999. *Speaking into the Air: A History of the Idea of Communication*. Chicago: University of Chicago Press.

Scannell, Paddy 1996. *Radio, Television and Modern Life: A Phenomenological Approach*. London: Blackwell.

Sconce, Jeffrey 2000. *Haunted Media: Electronic Presence from Telegraphy to Television*. Durham: Duke University Press.

Smulyan, Susan 1994. *Selling Radio: The Commercialization of Broadcasting, 1920-1934*. Washington: Smithsonian Institution Press.

Spigel, Lynn 1992. *Make Room For TV: Television and the Family Ideal in Postwar America*. Chicago: University of Chicago Press.

Spigel, Lynn & Denise Mann (eds.) 1992. *Television and the Female Consumer*. Minneapolis: University of Minnesota Press.

Spigel, Lynn & Michael Curtin (eds.) 1997. *The Revolution Wasn't Televised: Sixties Television and Social Conflict*. New York: Routledge.

Streeter, Thomas 1996. *Selling the Air: A Critique of the Policy of Commercial Broadcasting in the United States*. Chicago: University of Chicago Press.

Thompson, John B. 1995. *The Media and Modernity: A Social Theory of the Media*. Stanford: Stanford University Press.

Williams, Raymond 1974. *Television: Technology and Cultural Form*. New York: Oxford University Press.

Theoretical Reflections on Media and Media History

Niels Brügger

When one wants to reflect theoretically on media history, three fundamental questions immediately arise: 1) What do we understand by history? 2) What do we in fact understand by media? And 3) What then do we understand by media history? In the following, focus will primarily be placed on the second question, but the two others will be discussed briefly.

Historiography and the philosophy of history

Facing the question 'What do we understand by history?' one has to deal with the fundamental issues of historiography, that is, the well-known questions that any historian should address:

a) The question of the source material: How, where and in what condition do we find it? What is the validity of the sources? Are they representative? Are they primary or secondary? Are they non-symbolic or symbolic?
b) The question of interpretation: What are the limits of interpretation and to what extent does our contemporary view of the world work as a 'filter' on the past?
c) The question of disciplines that can help the historical study: psychology, sociology, archaeology, geography, demography, etc.
d) The question of the theories of history: How can we see and understand the conditions, the events and the processes of the past?

Besides these historiographical questions we also have to face the questions concerning the philosophy of history:

a) The question of the 'direction' of our history: When we turn the past into history, do we then give our history a direction? Do we see it for instance as a progress or a decline, or do we give our history no direction, which might mean that it is seen rather as a variety of transformations.

b) The question of the 'motor' of history: What are the driving forces of history?
c) The questions of periodisation: Should our history be divided into different 'slices' of time – and how do we do that? How short/long should they be? How distinctive are the ruptures?

These questions are some of the fundamental – and general – questions related to what we understand by history. Not that the answers to them are irrelevant to media history, they are indeed of great importance, also to the history of media. But since any history is the history of 'something', the essence of this 'something' must be discussed too.

Therefore, when one deals with media history one question still remains (no matter what the answers might be to the questions concerning history): 'What do we actually understand by media?' A question that is fundamental for the very simple reason that we have to know what the object of our historical studies is: What is our history about?

Media studies

The analytical object of media studies

'What do we understand by media?' can be approached in two different ways, which I shall call *ontological* and *epistemological*, respectively. The former discusses whether a certain artifact is – or is not – a media. This perspective seeks to set up a definition of media that can be used to determine whether a specific object deserves (or does not deserve) to be labelled 'media'. The latter takes a positive answer to the ontological question for granted: we agree that the artifact we are trying to study is, in fact, a media. The main concern of this approach is how we make this artifact into an *analytical object*, that is, an object for scientific study. So, when we want to answer the question 'what do we understand by media?' we can, on the one hand, try to determine whether an object is a media at all, or, on the other hand, aim to focus our studies of this object in a certain way.

In the following, the latter of the two possibilities will be addressed: what can media studies look at, when they want to study media – how to define the (possible) analytical object(s) of media studies? This of course applies to the historical studies of media as well.[1]

In order to give a satisfactory and exhaustive answer to this question one has to build upon some kind of theory, that is, a number of coherent propositions that can explain and clarify what we do when we study media, how we can at all turn media into scientific objects, and how this can be done in different ways. In other words: a general theory of media.[2]

The following pages can be considered the first steps in an attempt to develop a conceptual architecture for such a general theory of media. In this outline the key concepts are: media universe, mediacy, media matrix, configuration and reconfiguration.

Having said that, two reservations must be made. First, the following reflections are only concerned with theory and they are part of a work in progress. This means that their analytical impact has not yet been tested, and that they are not pretending to constitute a complete theory (both things have to be done in future works, hopefully in a fruitful interplay). In order to compensate for the 'abstractness' of the

1. In the article 'The Pursuit of Media History' the Norwegian media scholar Hans Fredrik Dahl also asks 'what exactly is the object of media history?' (Dahl 1994, 551). Is it communication (the communicative process and its effects) or is it the media (media as an institution, i.e. the communicative acts within a structure)? (op.cit., 556-60). The perspective that is to be outlined in the following tries to focus this discussion differently. First, there are more possible analytical objects to media history than just 'communication' and 'media as institutions'. Second, the following perspective does not reduce the study of media to a perspective that takes its point of departure at the institutional level. Third, it is argued that the (historical) study of communication must include a study of the media used for communication.
2. That it must be general means that it must not be media specific in its point of departure. A general theory should not take its point of departure in how one specific media is seen as an object for study – and then generalised. Rather than working outwards from a specific media, a general theory should aim at explaining as many media as possible.

following theoretical reflections, I have tried to illustrate some of the main points in a small excursus at the end of the article.

Second, the scope of this article does not allow for a more detailed and thorough discussion of the texts that have inspired me – and with which the following might be considered a critical dialogue (again, future works are needed). I would, however, like to mention the three traditions of media studies that I have in mind (all with a general and a historical perspective on media):

1) The Canadian tradition, above all Harold Innis, Marshall McLuhan and Paul Heyer,
2) The 'American section' of this tradition: Joshua Meyrowitz, Neil Postman, Carl J. Couch, Roger Fidler and Jay D. Bolter; and finally,
3) The tradition of the French *Annales school*: Lucien Febvre, Henri-Jean Martin, Jacques Le Goff, Michel Foucault, Patrice Flichy and Régis Debray.[3]

Media universe

Constituents, axes, elements, relations and configuration

The point of departure is what I have chosen to call the *media universe*. The media universe is a scematic representation of the 'universe' that a media will always be a part of and surrounded by, and in which the elements and their relations constitute the different analytical objects for media studies.[4]

3. Patrice Flichy and Régis Debray – and perhaps also Michel Foucault – are, strictly speaking, not part of the *Annales school,* although their fundamental ideas do have affinities with many of the theoretical positions of this tradition. In fact, the integral history of the three traditions and of their possible interplay is still to be written (for an analysis of the relation between the theories of Innis, McLuhan and Foucault, see Heyer 1988, 141-55).
4. On a general level a great deal of my inspiration for the following points about the media universe comes from the article 'Images of media' by Joshua Meyrowitz (Meyrowitz 1993 & Meyrowitz 1997 (an extended, Danish version of Meyrowitz 1993)).

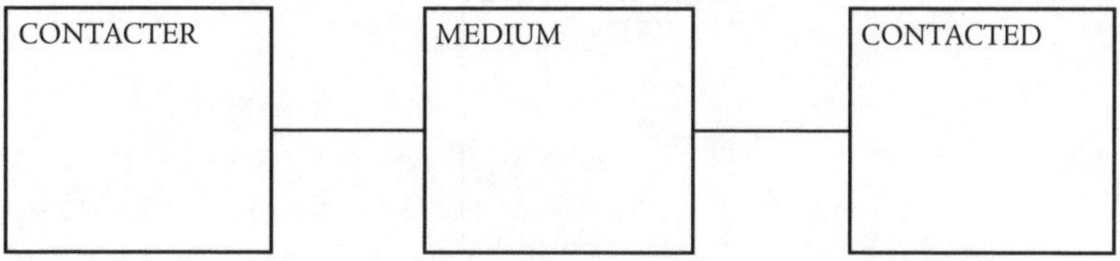

Fig. 1

The media universe consists of seven *constituents*, of which six are placed on two axes, and one is surrounding all the others. These constituents are articulated through different *elements* (or parts of elements). And between the various constituents and elements different *relations* will be possible. And finally: the constituents and the elements that articulate them as well as their relations constitute a *configuration*.[5]

The axis of contact: Contacter, medium, contacted

On the axis of contact we find three constituents: the contacter, the medium and the contacted (cf. figure 1).

This axis is explicitly *not* called 'the axis of communication' and these curious words 'contacter'/'contacted' are used instead of sender/receiver. This is done in order to insist on the fact that if media are means of communication of content from a sender to a receiver, they are means for contact before they are means used for communication. If one wants to do *media* studies, the point of departure must be the media, and not communication.[6]

5. This might sound more complicated than it is, but on a general level it is close to the model of actants, known from Greimas. 'Actant' is here called 'constituent', 'actor' is called 'element' (or part of an element), and, just like Greimas, I talk of axes and relations between actants/actors, constituents/elements.
6. This is also why the word 'media universe' is used instead of 'communication model'. As noted above the media universe is a schematic representation of the universe that 'follows' the medium, and therefore not a model of communication, trying to explain the phases/elements in a process of communication.

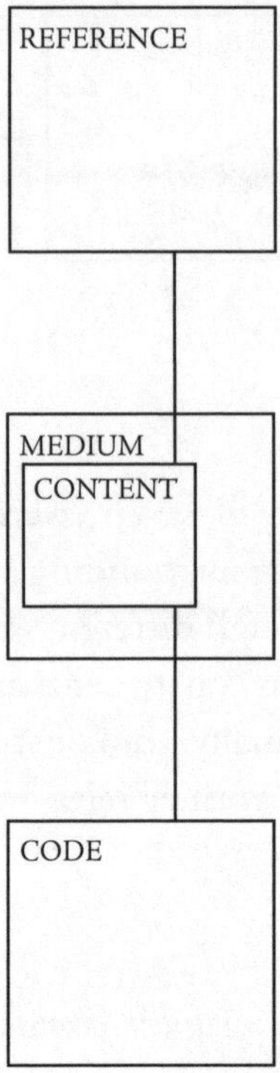

Fig. 2

Along this axis the contacter contacts the contacted through a contact, the medium. This way of seeing the medium emphasises that, basically, the medium should be seen as something that establishes a contact between two entities. In this sense one might say that medium means 'medium'– *in between*, and thereby something that creates a contact. Therefore the medium is the principal constituent – the *conditio sine qua non* – on this axis: no contact means no contacter/contacted (and no communication).

The possible analytical objects for (media) studies on this axis will be: 1) the medium, the contacter or the contacted in themselves; 2) the relations between: a) the medium and the contacter, b) the medium and the contacted, c) the contacter, the medium and the contacted (a few examples of concrete analytical objects are mentioned in the section 'Media History' at the end of the article).

The axis of presentation: Content, code, reference

On the axis of presentation we find three constituents: the content, the code and the reference (cf. figure 2).

This axis is explicitly *not* called 'the axis of representation' because it should be emphasised that first of all media present things, which *can* be said to re-present something. But the point of departure is that something is present (and thereby presented). The discussion of whether and/or how it re-presents might thus follow.

Along this axis the content presents the reference by the use of a certain code. In this sense the content is the principal constituent on this axis: no content means no code and no reference. But as mentioned above the content (with its code and reference) is always content within a medium, which again leads to the medium indirectly being the *conditio sine qua non* of the whole axis of presentation.

The possible analytical objects for (media) studies on this axis will be: 1) the content, the code or the reference in themselves; 2) the relations between: a) the content and the code, b) the content and the reference, c) the content, the code and the reference. And since the constituents on the axis of presentation are *in* the medium - and thereby in between the contacter and the contacted - the number of analytical objects for media studies increases. One could examine a network of relations, for instance: 1) contacter, content, 2) contacter, content, code, 3) contacter, content, reference, contacted, 4) contacter, content, code, reference, contacted, and so forth. And all of these relations plus their relation to the medium, that is: 1) contacter, content + medium, 2) content, contacted + medium, and so forth.

Context

The constituents on the axis of contact and on the axis of presentation are situated within the last constituent: the context (cf. figure 3).

The context can be studied on different levels on a scale between macro and micro. That is, between the 'societal' level, on the one hand, and the close and immediate surroundings of a medium, on the other.[7] And the elements within the constituent 'context' can relate to different fields (on both the micro and macro level). These fields could

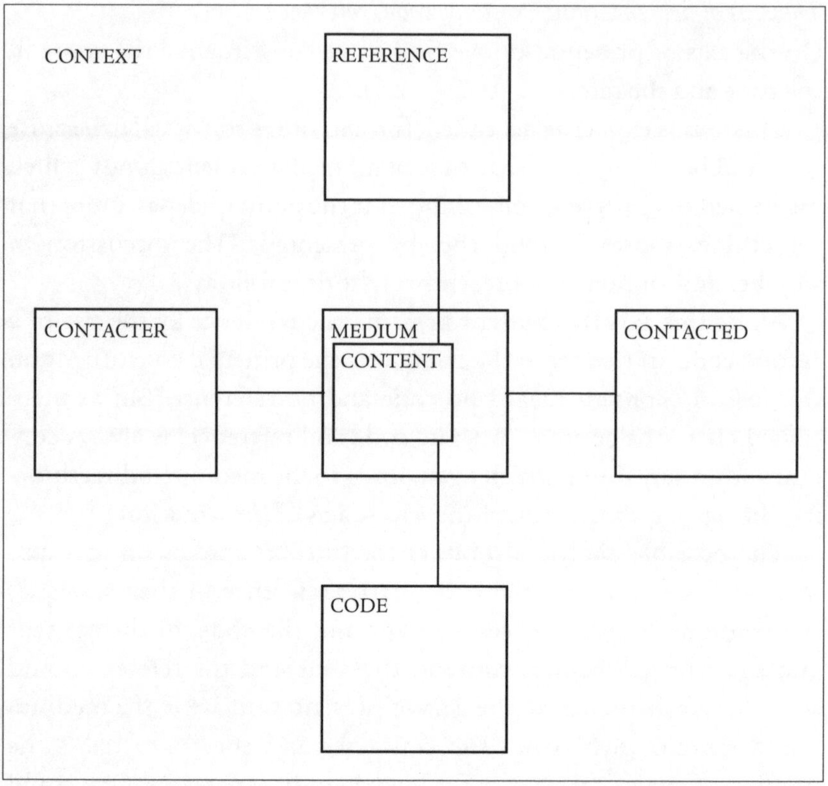

Fig. 3

be the political, the economic, the social/sociological, the cultural, the systems of ideas, the physical, other media, etc.[8]

The possible analytical objects for (media) studies in relation to the context will be: 1) the context itself; and 2) all the constituents and relations mentioned above in their relation to the context.[9]

7. My use of the terms macro and micro in relation to the context is indebted to Joshua Meyrowitz, although I use them differently. Meyrowitz talks of the context (or the environment) that the medium 'creates' or 'is' (cf. Meyrowitz 1993, 62), while I am talking of the context that surrounds the medium (and the other constituents).
8. As maintained earlier (note 6) the media universe is not a model of communication, but it does obviously have affinity to some of the well-known communication models, insofar as some of these have inspired the look of the media universe. The point of departure has been the communication model presented by the linguist Roman Jakobson (Jakobson 1960), but – apart from the fact that the media →

Media studies – studies of the medium?

In relation to all these possible analytical objects of media studies, a fundamental question arises: are they, in fact, all *media* studies? For instance, is the study of the *content* of a medium a *media study* in the strict sense of the word? I would argue, that if one studies the content of a medium as a closed entity, it is not *media study*; it is the study of content that 'happens' to be within a medium. If the content is studied 'in itself', without focusing on the relation to the medium that it is within, it is not part of media studies. To be so, the analysis must to some extent reflect upon the fact that the content is a *content within a medium*. That is, consider the relation medium/content. If it does not do so, it will be in danger of becoming the study of content in general (or e.g. literary studies, which can be both relevant and interesting, but which are not *media* studies). The same goes, of course, for the other constituents and relations. If audience or reception studies do not, for instance, reflect upon the fact that the content and the contacted and their relation are *content within – and contacted by – a medium*, they might be in danger of becoming pure ethnography or sociology, just as the economic or organisational study of the contacter might, for example, be in danger of becoming a pure economic or organisational analysis if it does not reflect upon the medium. To make such studies *media*

→ universe is not meant to be a communication model – the differences are: 1) only the constituents – called by Jakobson the 'constitutive factors of communication' – are maintained and not the 'functions of language', linked to each of the 'factors'; 2) other names are used for most of the constituents; 3) a seventh constituent is added – the context – that is to be distinguished from what Jakobson ambiguously calls 'context' (the 'reference' in the media universe). Here I follow the critical remarks to Jakobson by the anthropologist and linguist Dell H. Hymes, who proposes to include the whole situation surrounding the act of communication (cf. Hymes 1962, 25, 27, 31).

9. As stated earlier the main objective here is to define the possible analytical objects for media studies in a systematic way. How one wants to approach and explain each of these analytical objects (the elements on one (or more) constituent(s) and their relations) is not the subject. But the frames for these more detailed methodological and theoretical discussions within – and between – the different disciplines of media study could be the conceptual architecture outlined here.

studies they should deal with the specialness of the reception of this content, *because* it is content within and reception through a specific medium (with a specific being). And what is special about such an economic or organisational structure, when it is an economy or an organisation where a medium is at the centre? What role does it play for the economy or the organisation of public service broadcasters that the core of their production is related to a medium - television - and not to aeroplanes or hamburgers?

The only 'exception' to this is, of course, the study of the medium itself - a study that is necessarily part of media studies. So if a study of one of the six constituents of the media universe other than the medium itself wants to be a media study it must to some extent incorporate an analysis of the medium.

This does not mean, of course, that one should not do content analysis, reception analysis or production analysis, and so forth. And it does not mean that one should only do analysis of the being of the medium. What it means is, that one should do both: study the being of the medium and its relation(s) to the other constituent(s) that one wants to focus on.

The medium as frame setter

Can one say something, then, about this relation between the medium and the other constituents on a general level? I would argue that this relation could be understood as a *relation of frame setting*. The medium in its specific way of being (later called 'mediacy') sets up the frames - in the form of limitations and conditions of possibilities - for the other constituents and their interrelations (cf. figure 4).[10]

In this sense the specific being of a medium plays an important role for what kind of elements (or parts of elements) that can figure as contacter and contacted, how they can act, and what kind of relations they can establish. Just as it plays an important role for what kind of

10. The idea that the medium in its specific material being sets up frames for its 'use' is seen already in 1963 by the German media psychologist Gerhard Maletzke, although Maletzke uses a more 'deterministic' expression by talking of 'Zwang des Mediums' (Maletzke 1963, 39-41).

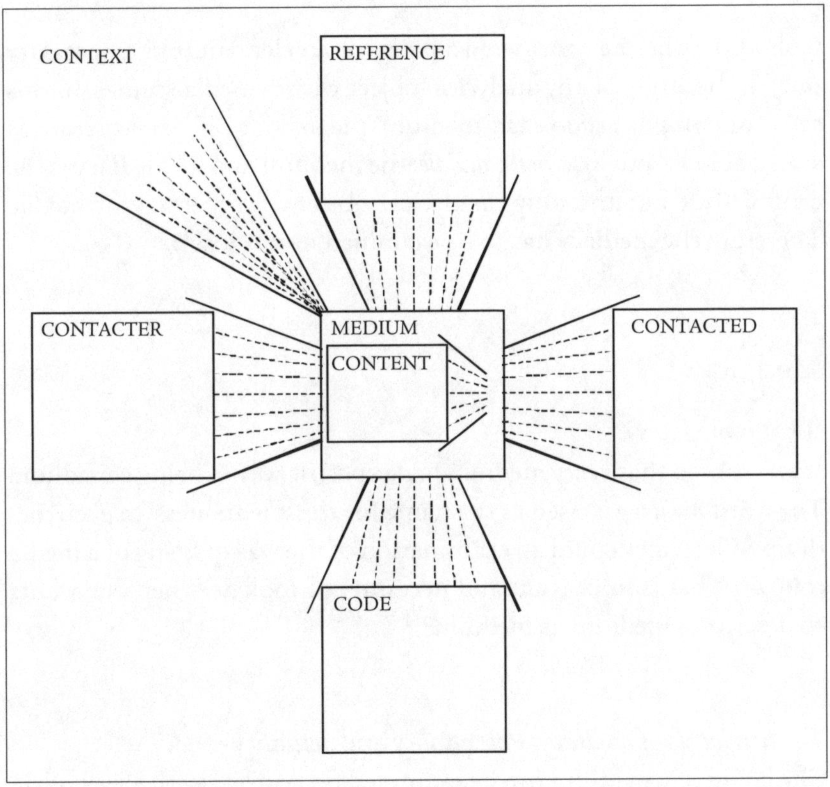

Fig. 4

elements that can figure as content, code, reference and context, how they can be, and what kind of relations they can have.

Mediacy: A double agent within media studies

In order to sum up this argument, one might say that the specific being of a medium – its mediacy – works as a 'double agent' among the analytical objects of media studies. On the one hand, the mediacy of the medium can be an independent analytical object for media studies, but, on the other hand, the mediacy of the medium must be considered an absolute necessity to any media study. Either one studies the mediacy in itself – an object that is clearly distinct from the other objects – or one studies the mediacy and its relation(s) to one (or more) of the other constituents that one wants to focus on. But it is important to stress that talking of mediacy as a *double* agent indicates, that the study of the mediacy in itself is not supposed to stand alone.

It should rather be considered a phase or an element (but a necessary one) in the study of any analytical object within media studies. In this sense one might argue that 'medium' means not only *in between* – as stated above – but also *in the middle*: the medium and its mediacy is the central (but not the only) analytical object of any study of media. Therefore the mediacy has to be examined more closely.

Mediacy

What is mediacy?

It is assumed that every medium has a specific way of being a medium. The word *mediacy* is used as the name for the 'media-ness' of each medium. What lines could an examination of the way of being of a media follow? What is important and necessary to look at, when one wants to describe a medium as medium?[11]

The two levels of mediacy: Potentiality and actuality

The being of a medium can be examined on two levels: the level of *potentiality* and the level of *actuality*.[12]

The potentiality is the outer poles that the material of the medium sets, and between which a field of possibilities is opened, i.e. where certain forms of the medium can be actualised. This is much

11. In Danish the word 'mediatet' is used. The Belgian media scholar Philippe Marion uses the word 'médiativité' to characterise the being or the ontology of a medium (cf. Marion 1993, 278; Marion 1996, 160-67; Marion 1997, 78-83; in French 'mediacy' would be 'médiaté'). The approach to media studies and the way to characterise the being of the medium that one finds in several of Philippe Marion's texts are in many ways close to the ones outlined in this article.
12. How these two concepts should be understood philosophically and how they can be applied to media is still to be discussed more thoroughly (for instance: what are their relations to the concrete artifacts? How can one 'see' the potentiality, etc.?). This is to be done by re-interpreting the genealogy of these concepts, from Aristotle and Thomas Aquinas over Leibniz and Schelling to Bergson and Deleuze).

like a volume adjusting dial on a radio, which can be turned from one extreme point to another, opening a field of possible positions between them.

The actuality is the way that a medium in a certain situation makes some (or all) of the potentialities actual. That is the actual point where the volume dial on the radio is placed (here only one element of the potentiality is made actual).

The consequences of this argument are that the medium, on the one hand, is what it is (actuality), but at the same time it is also more than it is (potentiality). Within the material limits of the medium there is room for changes – it can change, and yet remain 'the same', as long as the limits themselves are not changed; if they are we might have a new type of medium. Taking the volume dial again: it is always placed in one position, but it could have been placed in another position within its material limits. The question then is: what makes (historical) changes come about and what can make some of the potentialities actual?

The dialectic of mediacy

To answer this question one has to look at the medium as part of the media universe, that is the medium in its relations to the elements within the other constituents. It seems obvious that there is a *dialectic relation* between, on the one hand, the actual being of a medium in a certain situation (and indirectly its potentiality) and, on the other hand, the elements within the other constituents of the media universe (cf. figure 5).

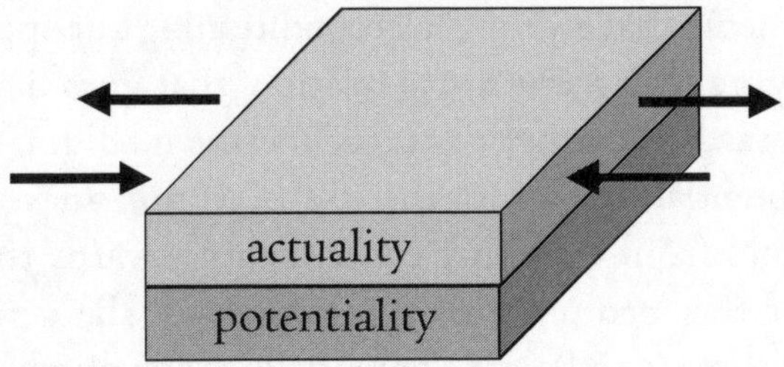

Fig. 5

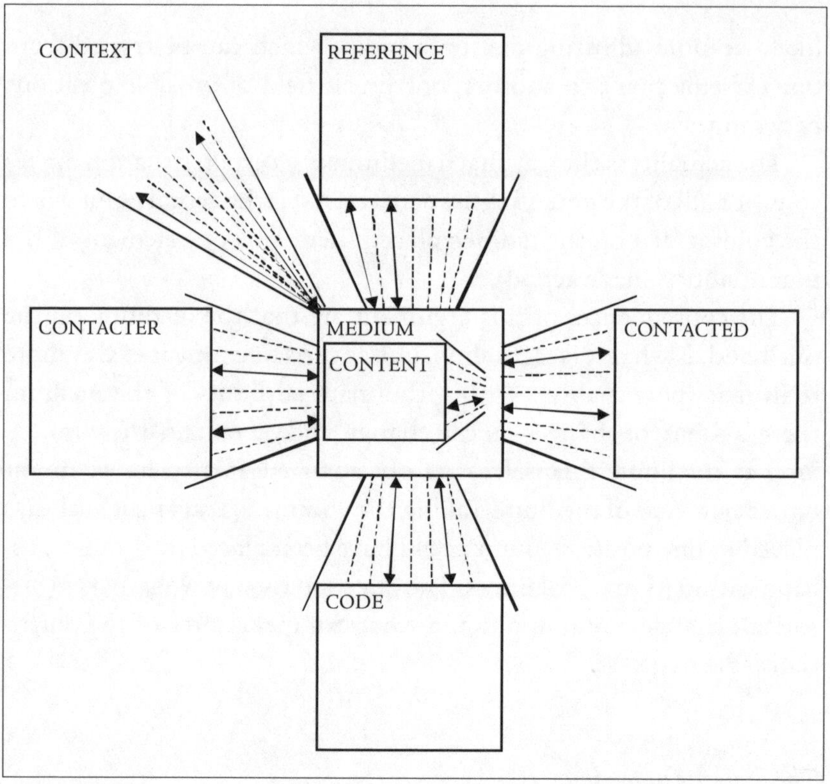

Fig. 6

The level of actuality (and indirectly the level of potentiality) constitutes a *condition* for the ways the other constituents can relate to the medium (the medium as frame setter), but the level of actuality is also a *result* of the ways the other constituents relate to the medium. Thus, the level of actuality is, at one and the same time, the condition for and result of the elements within the other constituents. On a general level what takes place between the medium and the other constituents are two movements that are mutually conditioning but opposite in direction (cf. figure 6): a *frame setting* relation, that goes from the medium 'out' towards the other constituents (the medium sets certain actual (and potential) frames for the 'use' of it), and an '*actualising*' relation, that goes from the other constituents towards the medium (every 'use' of the medium either 're-actualises' the actual frames and/or makes some (or all) of the potentialities actual, which changes the actual frames of the medium).

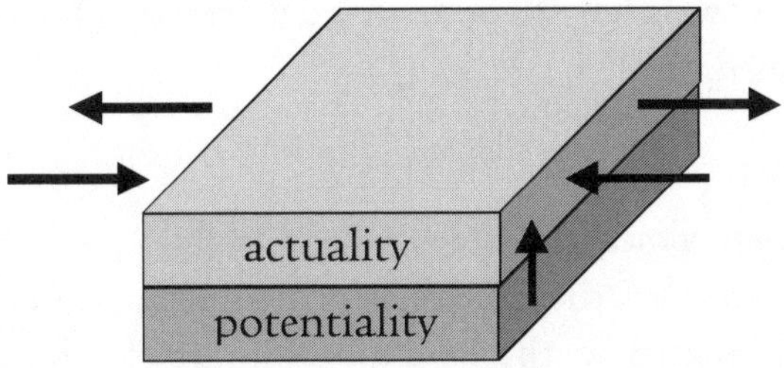

Fig. 7

Therefore, it is the mutual relations between the elements of the other constituents and the medium that causes changes at the level of actuality of the mediacy. These relations are, in themselves, not part of the mediacy but they can explain how changes of the medium come about.

Between the level of actuality and the level of potentiality the relation is different. Here one finds no dialectic relation, at least not in the sense just mentioned. The level of potentiality can *as such* not be changed by its relation to the level of actuality. One cannot change the volume dial's outer poles and the field between them just by using it. The material limits of the medium sets up a field of possibilities, giving room for the actual forms of the medium, but these limits cannot, as such, be changed as a function of the actualisations. This relation can therefore be described as a kind of 'dialectic', because there is interaction, but a 'one-way dialectic' because changes can only be brought about the one way – only the level of actuality can change (cf. figure 7).

However, this does not mean that the potentiality as foundation can never be changed; it just means, that it cannot be changed via specific ways of relating to the medium in a certain situation. But it can be changed from the 'outside', for instance if a part (or all) of the materiality of the medium is changed as such.

Let me sum up this point. The actual being of a medium is something that emerges out of the interplay between, on the one hand, a number of material limits and possibilities and, on the other hand, certain influences from the other constituents of the media universe. Therefore, the level of actuality is the level of changes within the medium, but both levels have to be analysed if one wants to describe the mediacy of a medium.[13]

The configuration of mediacy

After having described the two levels of the mediacy and their 'one-way' dialectical interplay, the next question arises: which type(s) of elements (or parts of elements) should be examined in order to give a satisfactory characteristic of the mediacy? Or as it was put earlier: what is important and necessary to look at, when one wants to describe a medium as medium?

I would argue that the elements within the constituent 'medium' can be placed in two interdependent categories (or two 'inventories'): *variables* and *areas*. These two categories are interdependent in the sense that they are merged: one or more of the variables will manifest itself within one or more of the areas (cf. figure 8).

The system that these variables and areas form in a specific medium at a specific time – both at the level of actuality and at the level of potentiality – is what one could call *the configuration of the medium*.

The variables of mediacy

As suggested earlier mediacy is closely linked to the materiality of the medium. This indicates that the matter of the medium plays a key role when one wants to determine the mediacy of a medium. I would argue that all of the following variables are a function of the matter of the medium; their way of being is made possible by the materiality of the medium. This, of course, does not mean that they *are* the materiality,

13. This distinction of two levels within the being of a medium is an attempt to avoid the tendency to media determinism that can be found in various degrees within the three traditions of media theory mentioned earlier. Instead of maintaining that print, radio or television are *always* this or that – and therefore will always have this or that psychological or societal effect – I would argue that these media are, in fact, this or that (the material being of the medium should, indeed, not be neglected), but only as a range of possibilities, opening a space for different 'uses', and therefore not always – and with necessity – having the same effects.

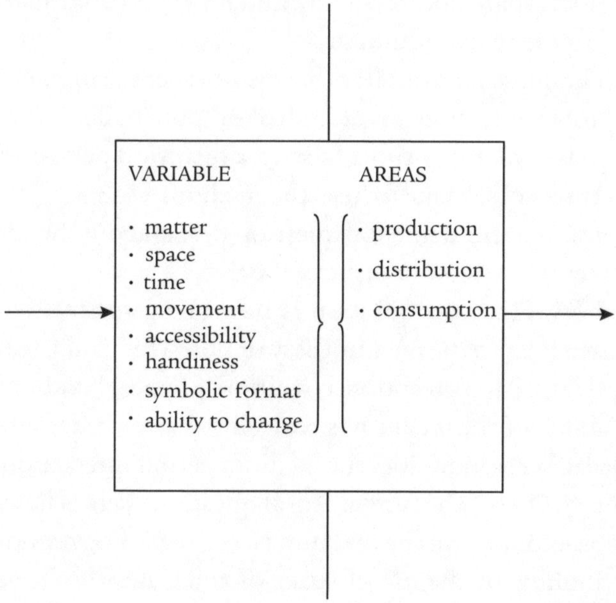

Fig. 8

that they can be identified with it. It rather means that they are not there if the material is not there and that the material 'bears in it' a certain 'interpretation' that makes the specific being of the other variables – and of their interplay – possible. In this sense this general theory of media could be considered 'media materialism'.

I would propose that, at least, the following eight variables should be included (the following variables might appear to be rather abstract; this is not intended in order to narrow down to more specific definitions, but to keep the categories on a very general level – at least as a point of departure).

1) *Matter*. The fundamental question of the *matter* of the medium is *whether* – and more precisely – *how*, it is physical or 'non-physical' (for instance micro-physical, electronic, energy-based...)? Part of this question could also be the weight: how light/heavy is the medium?
2) *Space*. The question to examine here is whether the matter of the medium 'interprets' space as 'extended' or 'punctual'. This could be, for instance, with regard to the dimensions/the volume (how

much/little space does it occupy, and how?). It could also be how it relates to the space around it.

3) *Time*. The question to address here is whether the matter of the medium 'interprets' time as 'extended' or 'punctual'. For instance, is the durability long or short (also in a historical perspective)? How much time does it take to 'use' the medium, etc.?
4) *Movement*. The fundamental question here is about the speed of the movement: how slow or fast can it be?
5) *Accessibility*. Here, the question is how one gets access to the medium: is access to the medium easy or not? This could, for instance, be with regard to perception, cognition, physical handling, etc. (the accessibility of the medium is basically what precedes interactivity, in a broad sense: how does the medium permit interaction with it?).
6) *Handiness*. One of the fundamental questions here is how economical/non-economical the medium is, i.e., regarding economy, physical handling, or the use of space or time? Another fundamental question linked to handiness is *easiness*: how easy is the medium to handle; this could be with regard to 'controllability', for instance.
7) *Symbolic format*. The fundamental question here is what kind of symbolic formats the matter of the medium is able to handle, that is, the 'alphabet(s)' of expression that the medium can use; these could be writing, non-moving images, moving images or sounds.
8) *Ability to change*. Here the fundamental question is whether the medium is dynamic or stable, and to what extent the materiality of the medium permits changes to any aspect of the medium?

The areas of mediacy

As referred to above the variables constitute one category among the elements within the constituent 'medium'. The other category contains the areas, and here three areas of the medium can be distinguished: production, distribution and consumption.[14]

14. It should be emphasised that these areas are areas *within* the medium. Therefore the word 'consumption' here does not mean the way the 'consumer' (the contacted) 'consumes' the media content, but rather the part of the medium that permits consumption, that makes consumption possible.

In order to elaborate these three, another distinction has to be introduced, namely, between *substratum* and *material content*. The substratum is the part of the medium on, or in, which the material content is placed. Taking the book as an example, the paper is the substratum and whatever is put on it (for instance black or coloured ink, or the like) is the material content, just as the substratum of the medium 'television' is the television set, and the illuminated dots of light (in black/white or colours) and the sounds that can be on/in it are the material content (at least concerning the consumptive part of that medium).

This distinction calls for two comments. First, the material content must not be confused with what has earlier been referred to as 'content' (that is the element within the constituent 'content'), but the two are, however, connected. As stated, the material content is the material part of what is on, or in, the medium, while the content (the element within the constituent 'content') is the 'meaning(s)' that might emerge out of or on the basis of the material content (from the perceptive recognition of colours, lines, forms, etc. to the constitution of meaning – according to which theory one uses to analyse the content). In this sense the material content is meaningless.

Second, the substratum must not be confused with the medium as such, but these two are also connected. The substratum is part of the medium, but only one part, the other part being the material content; in this sense, one might say that content is part of the medium (not as meaning, but as matter).

In order to summarise this point: the medium can be divided into three areas – production, distribution and consumption – and each of these can be divided into two components: substratum and material content. Therefore, trying to characterise, for instance, the area of production of a medium is to answer the following threefold question: what is the substratum of the medium, how does it make the production of material content possible, and what is this material content? The same goes for the two other areas, distribution and consumption: what is the substratum within the area of distribution, how does it make distribution of material content possible, and what is this material content that is now being distributed? Also, what is the substratum of the medium within the area of consumption, how does it make the consumption of material content possible, and how does this material content present itself for consumption?

One final remark has to be put forward about the three areas of mediacy. Maintaining that the study of a medium should include the areas of production, distribution and consumption means that the medium is studied very broadly: the whole circuit that the medium is – or is part of – has to be studied (the entities that ensure that the medium creates and maintains contact). Therefore, an exhaustive analysis of, for instance, the book as a medium cannot be limited to a description of the concrete artifact that we enjoy reading in our armchair. This is only part of the study, which has to include how the book was made as well as how it was able to reach us. The argument for this is that a medium should be studied as something that is in between a contacter and a contacted. But if focus is only on the book as an artifact that is either produced, distributed or consumed, it is not seen as something that is truly 'in between', but only as an artifact that is, above all, either produced (and not distributed/consumed), distributed (and not produced/consumed) or consumed (and not produced/distributed). Therefore, all three areas of a medium have to be studied – if not, only the copy of the book is studied, but not the book *as a medium*.

It should now be clearer as to how the variables and the areas within a medium are entangled. As referred to above the variables and the areas of the mediacy are interdependent in the sense that one or more of the variables will manifest itself within one or more of the areas. Within, for instance, the first area – production – this means that the substratum, the production of the material content in/on it and the material content itself, is composed by or takes place with the use of a certain matter that 'bears in it' a certain 'interpretation' of space, time and movement – a matter that can be accessed in certain ways, a matter that is economical/non-economical, easy to use, can handle certain symbolic formats and is dynamic or static. The same applies to the other two areas (it should be mentioned that, in many cases, the same material artifact will probably cover more areas).

Media types

Until now discussions about the mediacy of a medium have been on an 'abstract' level: the medium 'book', 'television', etc. Obviously, an analysis of the mediacy will have to take its point of departure in a specific, concrete artifact and not in an abstract media type. But even when this is done it will be no surprise that many specific, concrete artifacts do have things in common (most 'book artifacts' look like the medium type 'book'). Therefore, it might still be useful to talk of media types, but fundamental questions remain: how can it be determined whether a given artifact should be understood as this or that media type, and how can we determine the 'limits' of a media type? Talking of 'the mediacy of a medium', what precisely is meant by *a* medium? Should, for instance, the artifact e-book be understood as a book or as a personal computer? – or as an entirely new media type? And can the personal computer (with a connection to the internet) be understood as the medium radio? Etc.

My remarks on this point are not an attempt to give an answer to these specific questions – or to others like them – but rather to reflect upon how one can talk of media types at all, that is how we can focus a discussion on media types. I would propose a combination of, on the one hand, the ideas about categories and prototypes put forward by the linguist George Lakoff and the philosopher Mark Johnson (based upon the ideas of psychologist Eleanor Rosch), and, on the other hand, the ideas of mediacy mentioned above.

According to Lakoff and Johnson dining-room chairs and armchairs are prototypic chairs, while the beanbag chair and the barber chair are not prototypic, but nevertheless we categorise them as chairs, because they do have sufficient family resemblances to the prototypic chairs (cf. Lakoff & Johnson 1981(1980), 122). To Lakoff and Johnson at least three points are important in this perspective. First, being a member of a category is a question of degrees of resemblance to a prototype, and not a question of essence or inherent properties. Second, the members of a category share at least one property with the prototype, but this shared property does not necessarily have to be the same for all members of the category; there is no fixed core that all members must have. Third, the categories are open-ended, thus forming a kind of 'network'; things are not necessarily either inside or outside the category (cf. op.cit., 122-24).

When these ideas are applied to what has been said about the mediacy of the medium, it becomes possible to discuss whether a certain artifact should be seen as this or that type of medium, according to how many/few elements of its configuration of variables and areas it shares with prototypic members of the category in question. Such a perspective on media types might lead to the conclusion that the e-book can be understood as a book, but not as a prototypic book – or as a personal computer, but not as a prototypic computer. In the same way as the personal computer with an internet connection can be seen as a radio, but not as a prototypic radio, etc.

However, the ideas of Lakoff and Johnson cannot be used as they are in a discussion of media types. Especially the second point just mentioned is problematic ('all members of a category do not have to share one and the same property'). In fact, all members of the media category 'television' *must* share one element: the screen (at least within the area of consumption), just as all members of the media type 'radio' must be able to handle the symbolic format 'sound' (in the areas of production and consumption), and the media 'personal computer/internet' must be able to handle the symbolic format 'digital writing', etc.[15] (and this will probably be the case for all media types).[16] However, this does not mean that even if a given artifact does have this indispensable element, we will necessarily call it prototypic. So, apart from this limitation, my guess would be that talking about the elements of the mediacy of a medium in terms of prototypes, family resemblance and open-ended categories could be a fruitful way of discussing whether a given media artifact is or is not a certain type of media.

Media matrix

The media matrix and its dialectic

It was noticed earlier that one of the elements within the constituent 'context' could be another media. When this is the case, the whole media universe of one (or more) medium is part of the context for another medium, and vice versa (cf. figure 9).

15. Cf. Finnemann 1999, where the importance of this invariant trait by the computer has been analysed.
16. One might protest to Lakoff and Johnson that this could also be argued for chairs if you take a consumptive perspective: they must all be able to be sat on/in (cf. their discussion of 'interactional perspectives', op.cit., 123).

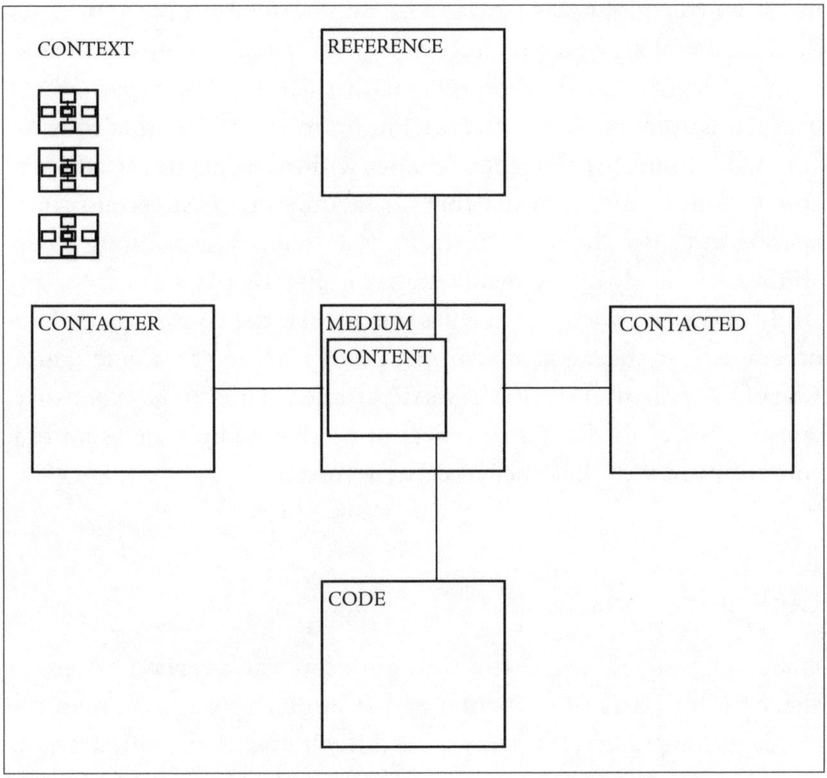

Fig. 9

This means that relations are established between all of the different constituents in both of the two media universes - or between all the co-existent media universes, at a certain time within a certain space. These relations are part of what I would call the *media matrix*.[17] By media matrix I understand the following two things: first, the number of co-existent media (and media universes) at a certain time within a certain space; and second, the dialectic between these media, i.e. the mutual conditioning that can be seen between all (or some) of the constituents within the specific media universes.

So in this sense a special analytical object for media studies would be the media matrix. In any media study that involves the context, the

17. Joshua Meyrowitz uses the expression 'media matrix' in *No sense of place* (Meyrowitz 1985, 69, 127-28, 339-40). I do not know if Meyrowitz is the first media scholar to use the expression, and I am not sure that I use it here in exactly the same way as he does.

media matrix might play a direct role. But for the study of the mediacy of a medium it *must* play a role, because the level of actuality of the mediacy emerges out of an interplay with the elements within all the other constituents. In other words: one (or more) of the other co-existent media could be the agent of change within the mediacy (unless, of course, one studies a media that is the only one at a certain time/space). And since the mediacy works as a double agent among media studies, the study of the media matrix indirectly plays a role for any study of media: when one studies one media, the co-existence of another media in the media matrix might be the reason for the actualisation of the potentialities in the media studied. Thus, to be exhaustive, any analysis of media has to reflect upon the medium in its mutual conditioning with the other co-existent media.

Configurations

It was suggested above that a configuration was a certain system of elements (or parts of elements) and relations between these in the media universe at a certain time. The different types of configurations that concern the mediacy can now be summed up:

1) The configuration of variables and areas within the *medium* at the level of potentialities;
2) The configuration of variables and areas within the *medium* at the level of actualities;
3) The configuration of all of the constituents within the *media universe*;
4) The configuration of the media universes among each other within the *media matrix* (a specific part of 3).

Media change

Reconfigurations: The dynamics of the media universe and of the media matrix

The four configurations referred to above are all seen from a static perspective: what are the configurations at a certain time? But one could also adopt a *dynamic* perspective, a perspective that focuses upon the changes between two configurations: how have they changed - and why have they changed? In other words, a study of the *reconfigurations*, which is the word I would like to use for such a study. How the configurations have changed should be analysed by examining how the elements within and the relations between the constituents of the media universes have changed. And regarding 'why they have changed', the question here is, whether one or more of the changed elements play a key role as the agent of change. Here the (re)configuration of the media matrix again might play an important role. Looking for the agent of change in relation to one of the configurations, any media study could with advantage examine the media matrix. But for the study of the changing of the mediacy, the media matrix must again play a key role, since the agent of change on the level of actuality of the mediacy can be an element within the constituent 'context'. This means that if one wants to point out some possible reasons for the change of one medium, one has to examine whether the media matrix has changed or not: has a new media (or part of media) been introduced - or has a co-existing media (or part of media) disappeared or changed?

As mentioned earlier, the study of the media matrix indirectly plays a role for any study of media, which also goes for the dynamic perspective of the study of reconfigurations.[18]

18. The idea of reconfiguration - that co-existing media affect each other - is not new. A genealogy of this concept should, at least, include the following: 1) Marshall McLuhan, using terms like 'interplay', 'reshape' and 'reconfigure' (McLuhan 1987(1964), 26, 52, 154, etc.); 2) Neil Postman, talking about 'resonance' (Postman 1985, 18, 41, etc.); 3) Joshua Meyrowitz using the expression 'effect loops' (Meyrowitz 1985, 173-83); 4) Régis Debray, talking about 're-inscribing' and 'reactivation' (cf. Debray 1996(1994), 17, 35, etc.); 5) Jay D. Bolter using the expression 'remediation' (cf. Bolter & Grusin 1999, 3-84); and 6) Roger Fidler for whom the key concept is 'mediamorphosis' (cf. Fidler 1997, 22-29). However, the concepts of these theorists do have limitations. When McLuhan, Postman or Debray talk of 'reshape', 'resonance' or 'reactivation' it is not quite clear which constituents and relations of the media universe that do have an effect upon another medium, or which constituents/relations that are affected. Bolter and Meyrowitz are in a way complementary, but not complete. Bolters concept of 'remediation' only →

Excursus – a short illustration

A classical analysis of the printed book in the 14th and 15th centuries, carried out by Harold Innis, can illustrate some of the points about the mediacy of a medium.[19]

Within the area of production, the matter of the printed book is described by Innis in these words:

> The use of oil in painting and its extension to ink, the development of an alloy which could be melted at low temperatures and remained consistent in size with changes in temperature, the growth of skill in cutting punches, the invention of an adjustable type mould, and the adaptation of the press were brought into a unified system as a basis for printing. (Innis 1991(1951), 23)

To this we have to add the substratum: paper and binding. This system of printing bears in it a range of potentialities (of which some are made actual) that concern more of the variables mentioned earlier. Let me just elaborate two of them:

1) The movement within the production could have been slow or fast, but actually it was fast, at least if compared to the production of the manuscript.
2) The dimension of the books (space) could have been both big and small, thus causing them to be either heavy and difficult to handle or light and easy to handle (handiness), but at the beginning of the printing era the actual size of books tended towards the large (heavy, uneasy), very much like manuscripts.

→ deals with the constituents/relations on the axis of presentation (remediation concerns the 'visual representations', cf. op.cit., 11, 24, 30, etc.), while the relations to the axis of contact and the context are left out. Talking of 'effect loops' Meyrowitz treats the relations on the axis of contact (op.cit., 173-80), as well as the relations to the context (social life outside the media, op.cit., 180-83), while the relations on the axis of presentation are left out. Fidler is the most 'complete' of the theorists mentioned.

19. This small digression serves here as an illustration; therefore it pretends neither to be exhaustive, nor to discuss Innis' analysis.

Within the area of distribution two things should be remarked. First, each copy of a book (the matter of the artifact) could have been transported by a slow or fast means and distributed locally or 'globally', but the actual size/weight of books meant that they were transported slowly and to nearby destinations. Second, that there were 'limited transportation facilities' (ibid.): the matter of the artifact in/on which the books were transported (horses, vehicles, roads, etc.) also tended to limit the size of the area to which books were distributed. All in all, the actual distribution of books was slow and limited to areas relatively close by.

One could say that these properties create a kind of 'tension' within the mediacy of the book between, on the one hand, the matter within the area of production that can be relatively fast, and, on the other hand, the matter within the area of distribution that is slow and limited to areas close to the place of production. This inner tension can become problematic if the societal/economic context of the book contains the element 'capitalist economy'. When this is the case the number produced – as well as the speed of both production and distribution – have to be increased in order to capitalise the investment; a demand that collides with the mediacy of the book. Production can be speeded up while distribution cannot, rapidly leading to a saturation of the local market. The 'solution', therefore, is to create new markets (ibid.). But since the matter in/on which the books are moved (vehicles, roads, etc.) cannot be speeded up significantly, another way is chosen in order to reach new markets: the artifact being moved is changed by making the size as well as the typography of the books smaller (and thus lighter and easier to handle; cf. 'the use of more compact type for smaller portable volumes in italics', ibid.). Now, a rapid distribution can correspond with the rapid production.

So, the material being of the book could vary between big/heavy/uneasy and small/light/easy (potentiality), but at the beginning of the printing era it actually was big, heavy and uneasy (actuality), and the possibility of making smaller books was neither 'seen' nor needed. But in an interplay with the elements of three other constituents – 'capitalism' as context, 'publisher' as contacter and 'market' as contacted – this hitherto 'unseen' – but possible – part of the material being of the book was made actual.

But is the size of books of any importance? Since the mediacy of a medium sets up the frames for the elements within and the relations to other constituents, the size of books is important, and such a shift must supposedly have had an impact on the whole media universe of the book. And according to Innis, it actually did, because new types of writers, content and codes did emerge when the books became smaller:

An enormous increase in production and variety of books and incessant search for markets hastened the rise of the publisher, an emphasis on commerce at the expense of the printer, and neglect of craftsmanship. As the supply of manuscripts in parchment, which had been built up over centuries had been made available by printing, writers in the vernacular were gradually trained to produce material. But they were scarcely competent to produce large books and were compelled to write controversial pamphlets which could be produced quickly and carried over wide areas, and had a rapid turnover. (ibid.)

So, the printed book always had the potential of being small/light/easy – and thus setting the frames for new elements within the other constituents – but this potential only became reality in a mutual interplay with elements within the other constituents.[20]

Media History

Possible analytical objects for a history of media

After having tried to answer the question 'What do we understand by media', it is now time to return to the question of media history. What are the theoretical implications for media history if the above outlined reflections are used to understand the 'something' that our history is about? What possible media histories can be written, according to how

20. It is well known that this is the beginning of the emergence of a new medium: the newspaper, being an even smaller version of the book than the pamphlet, and for a long time keeping several of the codes of the book, the consecutive pagination for instance. Thus, for several centuries the newspaper was a 'book' – but not a prototypic book – until it became a new type of medium.

we define and delimit our analytical object, the media?[21] Let me try to outline some of them, while keeping in mind that in all the studies mentioned the fundamental questions raised in the beginning concerning historiography and the philosophy of history must not be forgotten.[22]

Configuration/reconfiguration

First of all it should be emphasised that all the histories mentioned below could be historical studies of either the *configurations* at a certain time or of the *reconfigurations*. They could either adopt a static perspective, examining one configuration in the past (partially or all of it), or they could adopt a dynamic perspective, examining the reconfiguration of a configuration into another configuration in the past (partially or all of it).

The media universe of one media

The media universe of one media (television, book, newspaper...) can be studied in three different ways.

The element(s) within *the constituent 'medium'* can be studied in itself, thus writing the history of the mediacy. How is the configuration of the variables and the areas (actually/potentially) at a certain period in history – and how has it eventually changed? How is television, the book or the newspaper as a medium, and how have they changed?

Or one could study the element(s) within *one of the other constituents in itself and its relation to the mediacy of the medium* (because of the mediacy being a 'double agent'). This could, for instance, be a study of the contacter: how were television, book or newspaper producers, insofar as they used a specific medium with specific properties? How did the

21. A lot of the possible media histories mentioned below are already well documented in the literature of media history. Some are less well-researched, while others are still to be written.
22. The relevance to media history of the general questions concerning the study of history is discussed in Startt & Sloan 1989 and Higgs 1998. The media types in focus by Startt & Sloan are the press, film, radio and TV, while the contributions in Higgs take their point of departure in different kinds of computers.

contacters affect the medium by their use of it? And how have changes within the medium affected the producers and their ways of producing? A history that then has to be focused more precisely, according to what one wants to examine – and what methods/theories one wants to use for doing this (cf. note 9). Is it, for instance, the mind, the social behaviour or the organisation – or any other aspect of the contacter – one wants to focus on?

And the same, of course, goes for the other constituents. One could do a historical study of the content and the medium (what/how was the content of television – using for instance structural, semiotic, hermeneutic theories – and what role did it play that this was 'content' in television?). One could also study the code and the medium: how were the rules for putting content elements together (layout, montage, genres, etc.); how were they affected by the medium, and how have they changed? Or a study of the contacted and the medium: has it, for instance, changed the act of reading (as, for instance, a physical and/or mental process) that the material being of the newspaper has changed? Or a study of the context and the medium: what social/economic/cultural impact did a medium have, or how did the social/economic/cultural context affect the medium?. Etc.

A third object for historical study would be the element(s) and their relations within *more than one constituent in itself and their relation to the mediacy of the medium*. What/how was the content of television, how were the codes used in making the content, how did the codes and the content 'establish' the reference, what role did television as medium play in this, and how was all this 'understood' or used by the viewer? Or: what effect did the introduction of the footnote (code) in books (medium) play for the content and for the reading of books (contacter)? Etc.

The media matrix

As suggested above the media matrix can be studied as a specific version of the relation between a medium and its context. This is also the case in a historical perspective. Doing media history, one can study how the media matrix was within itself at a certain time (and eventually how it has changed). What effect (if any) did it have upon the media universes of the newspaper, or of the radio, that television was introduced, etc.?

And since the media matrix plays an important role for the mediacy of any medium - and since the mediacy of a medium is part of all of the studies mentioned above - the study of the media matrix could be said to play an indirect role in all these studies. What effect (if any) did the introduction of television have upon the codes, the content and the reading of the newspaper, etc.?

The genealogy of the theories of media

One final remark about a somewhat marginal - but maybe important - area within the history of media: the history of the *theories* of media. The general theory of media outlined here might also serve as a frame for the writing of a genealogy of the theories of media. Which theories have been used in certain periods to 'say' something about media? Which elements and/or which relations of the media universe have they put into focus? And how has this changed by the introduction of new theories of media?

The purpose of such a project should be double, one aimed at the history of media, another aimed at the theoretical work with media theory. On the one hand, earlier theories of media might actually have played a role for the media in the past (very often the different theories of media that support the scientific studies of content, media institutions or reception are also used by the producers, the theories thus being 'recycled' in content or media institutions and thereby indirectly becoming a possible object for media history). And, on the other hand, if one has the intention of developing new media theories today, this could be done as a *re-actualisation* of relevant existing theoretical elements, from today and from the past. And to do this, one has to have systematic historical knowledge of the similarities and the differences between theories of media. The conceptual architecture outlined above might also be a tool in such a project.

References

Bolter, Jay David & Richard Grusin 1999. *Remediation: Understanding New Media*. Cambridge, Mass.: The MIT Press.

Les Cahiers de Médiologie 4, 1997 ('Pouvoirs du Papier'). Paris.

Couch, Carl J. 1996. *Information Technologies and Social Orders*. New York: De Gruyter.

Dahl, Hans Fredrik 1994. The Pursuit of Media History. *Media, Culture & Society* 16(4), 551-63.

Dahl, Hans Fredrik 2000. Den mediehistoriske metoden – finnes den? *Norsk medietidsskrift* 7(2), 60-71.

Debray, Régis 1991. *Cours de Médiologie Générale*. Paris: Gallimard.

Debray, Régis 1996(1994). *Media Manifestos: On the Technological Transmission of Cultural forms*. London: Verso.

Debray, Régis 1997. *Transmettre*. Paris: Odile Jacob.

Debray, Régis 1998. Histoire des Quatre *M*. *Cahiers de Médiologie* 6, 7-24.

Duguid, Paul 1996. Material Matters: The Past and Futurology of the Book. Geoffrey Nunberg (ed.), *The Future of the Book*. Berkeley: University of California Press.

Febvre, Lucien & Henri-Jean Martin 1976(1958). *The Coming of the Book: The Impact of Printing 1450-1800*. London: New Left Books.

Fidler, Roger 1997. *Mediamorphosis: Understanding New Media*. Thousand Oaks, California: Pine Forge Press.

Finnemann, Niels Ole 1999. *Thought, Sign and Machine: The Computer Reconsidered*. Aarhus:
www.au.dk/cfk/DOCS/PUB/nof/TSM/abstract.html

Fledelius, Karsten 1989. Audio-Visual History: the Development of a New Field of Research. *Historical Journal of Film, Radio and Television* 9(2), 151-63.

Flichy, Patrice 1995(1991). *Dynamics of Modern Communication: the Shaping and Impact of New Communication Technologies*. London: Sage.

Foucault, Michel 1973(1966). *The Order of Things: an Archaeology of Human Sciences*. New York: Vintage Books.

Foucault, Michel 1976(1969). *The Archaeology of Knowledge*. New York: Harper and Row.

Foucault, Michel 1979(1975). *Discipline and Punish: Birth of the Prison*. New York: Vintage Books.

Gumbrecht, Hans Ulrich & K. Ludwig Pfeiffer (eds.) 1994. *Materialities of Communication*. Stanford: Stanford University Press.

Heyer, Paul 1988. *Communications and History: Theories of Media, Knowledge, and Civilization*. New York: Greenwood Press.

Higgs, Edward (ed.) 1998. *History and Electronic Artefacts*. Oxford: Clarendon Press.

Hymes, Dell H. 1962. The Ethnography of Speaking. Thomas Gladwin & William C. Sturtevant (eds.), *Anthropology and Human Behaviour.* Washington D.C.: Anthropological Society of Washington.

Innis, Harold Adams 1991(1951). *The Bias of Communication*. Toronto: University of Toronto Press.

Innis, Harold Adams 1986(1950). *Empire and Communications*. Victoria: Press Porcépic.

Innis, Harold Adams 1952. *Changing Concepts of Time*. Toronto: University of Toronto Press.

Jakobson, Roman 1960. Concluding Statement: Linguistics and Poetics. Thomas A. Sebeok (ed.), *Style in Language*, Cambridge, Mass.: The MIT Press.

Jensen, Klaus Bruhn 1998. Hvad man ikke ved: Dagsorden for forskning i (dansk) mediehistorie. *Nordicom Information* 20(1-2), 27-36.

Lakoff, George & Mark Johnson 1981(1980). *Metaphors We Live by*. Chicago: The University of Chicago Press.

Lardellier, Pascal (ed.) 1999. *Histoire et Communication*. Paris: L'Harmattan.

Le Goff, Jacques 1993(1957). *Intellectuals in the Middle Ages*. Oxford: Blackwell.

Lenoir, Timothy 1998. Inscription Practices and Materialities of Communication. Timothy Lenoir (ed.), *Inscribing Science: Scientific Texts and the Materiality of Communication.* Stanford: Stanford University Press.

Maletzke, Gerhard 1963. *Psychologie der Massenkommunikation*. Hamborg: Verlag Hans Bredow-Institut.

Martin, Henri-Jean 1994(1988). *The History and Power of Writing*. Chicago: The University of Chicago Press.

Meyrowitz, Joshua 1985. *No Sense of Place: The Impact of Electronic Media on Social Behavior*. New York: Oxford U.P.

Meyrowitz, Joshua 1993. Images of Media: Hidden Ferment - and Harmony - in the Field. *Journal of Communication* 43(3), 55-66.

Meyrowitz, Joshua 1997. Tre paradigmer i medieforskningen. *Mediekultur* 26, 56-69.

McLuhan, Marshall 1995(1962). *The Gutenberg Galaxy: The Making of Typographic Man*. Toronto: University of Toronto Press.

McLuhan, Marshall 1987(1964). *Understanding Media: The Extensions of Man*. London: Ark Paperbacks.

Marion, Philippe 1993. *Traces en cases: Travail graphique, figuration narrative et participation du lecteur*. Louvain-la-Neuve: Académia-Erasme.

Marion, Philippe 1996. Propositions pour une Médiatique narrative appliquée: Lecture d'un reportage photographique de Paris Match. Jan Baetens & Ana Gonzalez (eds.), *Le Roman Photo.* Amsterdam: Rodopi.

Marion, Philippe 1997. Narratologie médiatique et médiagénie des récits. *Recherches en communication* 7, 61-87.

Pellegram, Andrea 1998. The Message in Paper. Daniel Miller (ed.), *Material Cultures: Why Some Things Matter.* London: UCL Press.

Postman, Neil 1985. *Amusing Ourselves to Death: Public Discourse in the Age of Show Business*. New York: Viking.

Schudson, Michael 1991. Historical Approaches to Communication Studies. Klaus Bruhn Jensen & Nicholas W. Jankowski (eds.), *A Handbook of Qualitative Methodologies for Mass Communication Research.* London: Routledge.

Startt, James D. & Wm. David Sloan 1989. *Historical Methods in Mass Communication*. Hillsdale, New Jersey: Lawrence Erlbaum.

Tacchi, Jo 1998. Radio Texture: Between Self and Others. Daniel Miller (ed.), *Material Cultures: Why Some Things Matter.* London: UCL Press.

Ward, Ken 1989. *Mass Communications and the Modern World.* London: MacMillan.

Winston, Brian 1995. How are Media Born and Developed? John Downing, Ali Mohammadi & Annabelle Sreberny-Mohammadi (eds.), *Questioning the Media: A Critical Introduction.* London: Sage.

The Change of News Structure

Danish Newspapers 1873-1914

Søren Kolstrup

Allan Bell

In *The Language of News Media* Allan Bell presents a rather short piece of news taken from *the Washington Chronicle* of 10th December 1876 (Bell 1990, 173). This text, covering a railway accident, has a totally linear and chronological structure. Bell makes a short comment about this and refers to Michael Shudson, according to whom reporters moved from recorders or stenographers to interpreters around the turn of the century. On the preceding pages Bell has given us a short introduction to the non-chronological order of the elements of the press story and the repetition of elements. A structure that van Dijk has described with the words 'top-down', 'relevance' order, 'instalment', commonly known as the inverted pyramid (cf. van Dijk 1988, 48). But as *The Language of News Media* is not a historical book, this is what Bell has to tell us about one of the most extraordinary changes in textual structures that western culture has seen since Gutenberg.

This paper tries to shed some light on the changes in the press in Denmark. What I present is an explorative investigation based on 2250 articles taken from 63 Danish newspapers covering the period from 1873 to 1914.

Time and History: Short-term, medium-term and long-term? The example of the popular press

The popular press of the 19th century and the beginning of the 20th century has been treated by media research as a stepchild. This is the thesis of Ulrich Lehrmann in his article on the popular press (cf. Lehrmann 1999, 47). I agree.

What we can read about this press in most texts (there are not that many) about Danish media in the 19th century is rather strange: The popular press rises and vanishes several times during the century, the most dramatic rise and fall occuring in the period 1890-1910. The history of the popular press is repetitive, cyclical. It is not a press in its own right, it is a tumor on the body of the true press – maybe, as Lehrmann suggests, this is because the history has been written by the victor: the omnibus press (cf. Lehrmann 1999, 47). The popular press is granted life (and death) by the true press. Its coming and passing has condemned it to a short-term history, or, at best, a medium-term history. The popular press has the right only to be the theme of a history of events: 'The rise and fall of Johannes Hansen, director of *Forposten/ Middagsposten*'. The history of the popular press has, up until today, been a history of institutions and almost nothing but that.

But the history of the popular press could just as well be seen in the light of long-term history, 'la longue durée' as the French historian Fernand Braudel puts it (cf. Braudel 1996(1969), 15-38). If we define 'popular press' not according to institutions (with their sometimes short lives), but according to its subject matter, to its themes, to the needs it fulfilled, to its functions, to its public, we would get a new history pretty close to the history of mentalities, the history of the popular newspaper reading material. Then we would get a history of a surprising stability: Crimes, scandals, sex, accidents, catastrophes, and personal attacks. Of course there would be variations over time, but not fundamental changes or breaks. We would then realise that there were fewer differences between popular press and the political press than we think – even the political press was filled with stories of crimes and scandals. On 6th February 1901, the popular newspaper, *Forposten*, talks about perverted sexual scandals on the Island of St. Thomas, but Sabroe's journalistic campaigns in the provincial labour paper *Demokraten* contained a good deal of that too; I am referring here to the 'Hebron campaign' of 1908 in *Demokraten*. Here the journalist Sabroe denounced the horrifying treatment of young girls who were undergoing reformative training in the Hebron borstal, and he made an outstanding social reportage that changed the lives of young people in such institutions. However, in this campaign he drew a severe portrait of the female principal of the Hebron borstal as a hypocrite, pervert and sadist lesbian. *Democraten* had quite a lot in common with the popular press. The popular press may come and go, but the popular stuff remains.

In *Ecrits sur l'histoire*, Fernand Braudel refers to his predecessor at Collège de France, Lucien Fèvre, who wrote the magnificent study *Rabelais ou le problème de l'incroyance au 16ème siècle*, an exploration of the mental tools of French thinking in the 16th century (and before). Lucien Fèvre proved, after 500 pages that in the 16th century it was impossible to be an atheist as the world could only be understood in religious terms throughout the whole of that century. One or two centuries more were necessary to make this 'atheist understanding' possible. Of course the historical actors of the 16th century attacked their opponents by calling them atheists. The description of this change is a true long-term history (cf. Braudel 1996 (1969), 15–38).

On the opposite side we have the stories (histories?) of Cavling. Cavling was the chief editor of the liberal intellectual newspaper *Politiken* from 1905 to 1913. In 1905 he changed the newspaper's format and to some extent its content by giving more importance to the use of reportage. The descriptions of these changes are normally rather anecdotal and are at best a short-term history: A history of institutions such as the newspaper *Politiken*. This appears clearly in *Medier og Kultur*, where the reader is confronted with a copy of the front page of *Politiken* from the 26th of April and from the 16th of May 1905 (cf. Drotner 1996, 47). Obviously there was a break of format/size and layout, but there was no revolution. *Politiken* went from 4 pages in 'blanket' format to eight or ten pages of broadsheet. The ads had disappeared from the front page, the layout was clear. In fact *Politiken* returned to a format and layout very like its layout in 1884 except for the disappearance of the ads from the front page (which were rather few in 1884!) but also with larger headlines even if still only covering one column. *Politiken* blended its old format with newer trends in layout. Thus the seemingly rapid change in *Politiken* in 1905 was only the manifestation and temporary end to a long and slow movement, and it was only first in 1905 that these changes - with historical roots as far back as the 1870s - became publically evident. This is the opinion of Søllinge & Thomsen in *De danske aviser 1634-1989* where the authors admit that Cavling's performance was a combination of elements that had already existed for a long time in Danish journalism (Søllinge & Thomsen 1989, vol. 2, 75).

This paper proposes to investigate a movement that has been very slow and whose beginning is difficult to grasp: the changing structure of the central newspaper genre: the news story, the genre that defined the newspaper as opposed to casual leaflets. It is at least a medium-term history - if not a long-term history.

The identity of the news genre

We all know that it is hard work to define the journalistic genres, what do they have in common and what distinguish them from each other, what are the criteria? But it is even worse to define them over time, what is the identity of a changing genre? Most books about journalism have a chapter on journalistic genres or text types. Normally the production processes are a fundamental criterion for defining genres; normally the definitions are very loose also, and the genre problem as such is admittedly not very important (see Meilby 1996, 64-72). News is the hardest genre of all - it can be anything! We cannot use structural features - they change. We cannot use the routines of the working process; even if that is the way most handbooks in journalism define the different genres. The elaboration of news stories has changed. The size is not a useful criterion: What is considered as a notice today was considered to be a rather long article 200 years ago. In the absence of any other criterion we have to admit that news can best be defined by its content, by the referent. News contains a rupture: Events that distinguish themselves from the daily routine are news (for more information about news as a rupture see Jamet & Jannet 1999a and 1999b). This has been a constant feature since the newspapers began. So news comprises crime, sex, scandals, accidents, marriages, catastrophes, political matters, etc. The content of news seems to have remained stable since the 16th century! In the late 19th century news contained equally all kinds of meetings, especially political meetings. The meeting was a rupture in the daily routine. The meeting was the instrument of political and social change. The meeting was news, was life. That is why reports of meetings were so important and that is why they were not from the outset excluded from news. Thus events like those mentioned above are always news.

Linear and non-linear principles in newspapers' layout

In 1850 linear principles reign not only in newspapers' layout but also within the single articles. This means that the newspaper invites the reader to a continuous reading line and that the story tells events in a chronological order. This 'continuous reading' model began on page 1, top left-hand column, and in 1850 there were still no headlines for each article, the specific news item not being an independent unit.

The few headlines that existed indicated the provenance of news, i.e., (a) the specific place from where it came, the newspaper (foreign or from a neighbouring town) that was the source of the information, (b) the mode of transport: Postal information and later telegram news, and (c) division into foreign countries ('Udlandet') and Homeland ('Indland/Fædrelandet'). In this case there was a thematic indication, which was closely related to the indication of the source.

Let us now consider the evolution of the newspaper from a layout of uninterrupted columns to that of a topographical or geographical display?

From the beginning of the 19th century newspapers looked like a book (with the same format as a book) and normally with two columns, but in the case of *Politievennen* there was only one. From the beginning of the century there were two formats: the square format and rectangular format but both were like books. In the 1840s Danish newspapers still had typically only two columns and they continued to have a pagination covering a whole year. The news stories were organised according to the principle of provenance. A single news item was thus not an independent unit, and even a particular issue of a newspaper was, in principle, not independent.

Aar 1815. Aarhuus Stifts No. 35.

Kongelig allene privilegerede

Adresse-Contoirs Tidende

som forsendes med Brevposterne.

Tirsdagen den 21de Marts.

Napoleon

er ikke længere paa Elba. Med væbnet Haand er han uforventet trængt ind i det sydlige Frankrige. Om denne høist imponerende Nyhed havdes i Wien, Berlin, Paris og London følgende Efterretninger:

Den afsatte Keiser havde den 26de Februar indbuden Kommandeuren for det ved Elba krydsende engelske Krigsskib, Admiral Campbell, til sit Middagstaffel. Efter ophævet Taffel blev han indespærret i et afsides Værelse; imidlertid gik Napoleon under Seil med sin Korvette. Af hans Tropper har han medtaget 1200 Mand Franskmænd, Polakkere og Korsikanere, fordeelte paa forskiellige Transportskibe og forsynet med megen Munition og med Levnetsmidler paa 6 Dage. Hvorledes alle disse Anstalter saa ubemærket ere kunne blevne trufne, er en uopløselig Gaade. Paa Portoferrajo har Napoleon efterladt sig en Garnison af 150 Mand og udnævnt Præfekten til Kommandant. Han er landet i Nærheden af Frejus. Efter at have udstædt en Proklamation til det sydlige Frankriges Indvaanere, skal Han allerede have sat sig i Besiddelse af den vigtige og faste Krigshavn Toulon, og hele Naboeprovindsen Savoyen, skal have paasat den trefarvede Kokarde. Hans Moder og Søster har han med sig. Hvor Napoleon egentligen selv var vidste man ikke bestemt, da Alt hidtil var skeedt i den kommanderende Generals Navn. — Man vil vide, at Napoleon staaer i nøie Forbindelse med Kong Joachim. — Han er af den franske Regiering erklæret for fredløs.

Frankrige.

Alles Opmærksomhed er henvendt til Rigets sydlige Provindser, og dette vil og være Tilfældet i hele Europa endog i dets fierneste Dele Napoleons Landgang er Gienstanden for Alles Underholdning. Kongen er meget rolig. Hs. M. har modtaget det diplomatiske Korps med megen Værdighed. Til de fremmede Gesandtere skal han have sagt: „Mine Herrer! tilmeld deres respektive Hoffer, at Bonapartes latterlige Forsøg, ikke mindre vil forstyrre Europas Rolighed, end den han forstyrret min Siels. — „I Krigsdepartementet hersker paa engang den største Virksomhed. En Mængde Tropper ere fra alle Kanter befalede til Opbrud mod Syden. Mellem Chamberi og Lion oprettes en Leir. Monsieur er allerede afreist for at overtage Kommandoen af denne Armee. Ved Grenoble staaer en betydelig Hær under General Miollis. Fra Marskal Massena har Regieringen havt Depescher, der melde Napoleons Landing og tillige hans frugtesløse Angreb paa Antibes; Staden Marseille har reist sig i Masse for at afslaae ethvert Angreb. Overalt besieles Folket og Autoritæterne af den bedste Aand mod Kongen. Tvendegange daglig holdes Statsraad.

Man trøstede sig i Paris med at det inden faae Dage vilde være afgiort med Napoleon; alle Forholdsregler ere trufne dertil, saavelsom og, for at kiende de Medforbundne. Paa mange og især paa en vis Marskal holder Regieringen et vaagent Øie, da man vil have opdaget at han nogle Dage før Publicum vidste noget om Napoleons Landgang, ved en som Fruentimmer forklædt ung Korsikaner havde erholdet Depescher fra ham. Bemeldte Marskals Hengivenhed for Napoleon giør hans Deeltagelse i denne Affaire høist sandsynlig.

Ved et den 7de Marts udkommen Kongeligt Dekret bliver Napoleon Buonaparte erklæret for Forræder og Rebel, fordi han med væbnet Haand er trængt ind i Vardepartementet. Det paalægges alle Øvrighedspersoner og Borgere at arrestere ham, og stille ham for en Krigsret, for at straffes efter Lovene. — Alle de Militairpersoner, som have fulgt ham ved sit Indfald i Frankrig, som og Alle, der ere i Forstaaelse med ham, eller ved Ord og Gierning søge at afstedkomme Borgerkrig, skulle straffes paa samme Maade.

Fra Statsministeren Grev Desolles er udstædt følgende Dagsbefaling:

Fig. 1. *Aarhuus Stiftstidende.* 21st March 1815

As it can be seen in figures 1 and 2, the main information – the pogroms in Copenhagen – has no title or headline! Two official declarations or announcements related to the affair have the title 'Declaration'; a royal announcement about knighthood orders (Riddere af Dannebrog); and finally at the end of column two, the headline 'Postal information'. The remaining information (on page two!) is organised according to the location (town) from whence the information came.

Onsdag
8 September

Dagen

No. 214
1819.

Redigeret af D. Didrichsen, Justitsraad.

Forlagt af Anne Marie salig J. P. Rostocks Enke. Trykt hos Brødrene Rostock.

Forsendes, i Følge Kongelig allernaadigst Tilladelse, med Pakkeposterne i Danmark og Hertugdømmene.

* * *

Den Aand, som paa adskillige Steder i Tydskland har viist sig mod Bekiendere af den mosaiske Troe, synes ogsaa nu at ytre sig hos os.

Løverdagen den 4de dennes om Aftenen var Folkestimmelen paa Østergade usædvanlig stor, og nogle Vinduesruder bleve slaaede ind hos tvende der boende Handelsmænd.

Politiet, som igiennem forskiellige Kilder var underrettet om, at saadan Folkestimmel kunde formodes, bragte det, understøttet af det Militaire, snart dertil, at alt inden Midnat var roligt.

Næste Dag giorde Politiedirecteuren ved en Placat Enhver opmærksom paa sine Pligter som Undersaat og Borger. Om Aftenen fornyedes imidlertid Folkestimmelen atter i den samme Gade; og skiøndt den offentlige Magt i det Øieblik, da der blandt Mængden sporedes Uroestiftere, ryddeliggiorte Gaden, kunde det dog ikke forhindres, at nogle faade og ildesindede Mennesker, som vankede om i de forskiellige Dele af Byen, tillode sig, understøttet af Mørket, at slaae Vinduerne ind i endeel Huse, hvor Personer af den mosaiske Troes Bekiendelse formodedes at boe, og at begaae andre slige Excesser.

Hans Majestæt Kongen lod derpaa den 6te udgaae en Bekiendtgiørelse, hvorved enhver blev advaret om, under Lovens Straf, at vogte sig for enten at deeltage i Uordener, eller at komme nær de Steder, hvor Sammenrottelse og Opløb fandtes; ligesom Allerhøistsamme og bemyndigede Politiedirecteuren til ved en Placat at udlove betydelige Summer til Belønning for Opdagelse af dem, der havde enten stiftet denne Uroe eller deeltaget i samme. Derhos blev Politiets Kraft forøget ved betydelig Assistence saavel af Borgercorpset som af det egentlige Militaire.

Disse kraftige Foranstaltninger kunne ikke forfeile deres Øiemeed.

Om Aftenen den 6te og 7de sporedes mindre Uroe. Nogle faa, som tillode sig lovstridige Foretagender eller viiste Trodsighed mod den offentlige Magt, bleve anholdte; og disse tilligemed flere forhen Anholdte, der samtlige høre til den allersimpleste Classe, vente nu deres Dom ved en i det Øiemeed nedsat Commission, der endog er bemyndiget til at dømme uden Appel.

Saaledes tør man vente Orden og Rolighed atter tilveiebragt ved de fra offentlig Side trufne Foranstaltninger. Og den gode Stemning Stadens Indvaanere ved denne, som alle andre lignende Leiligheder har viist, er Borgen for, at hine Optrin ikke ville blive fornyede.

Bekiendtgiørelse fra Politiedirecteuren.

Hans Majestæt Kongen har, i Anledning af de urolige Optrin, som den 4de og 5te d. M. have fundet Sted her i Staden, befalet mig at udlove en Belønning af 4000 Rbd. Sedler for den eller dem, som beviisligen opgive den, der enten har forfattet eller opslaaet noget af de Skrifter, hvorved der er offentligen bleven opfordret til voldsom Adfærd, eller hvem der som Hovedmænd har virket til, eller anført Hoben ved de foregaaede Uordener; samt en Belønning efter Omstændighederne fra 200 Rbd. til 1000 Rbd. Sedler for beviislig Angivelse af nogen anden, som har taget Deel i de foregaaede voldelige Handlinger. Angiveren kan desuden giøre Regning paa, at hans Navn vil blive fortiet.

Kiøbenhavns Politiekammeret den 6te September 1819.

O. H. Hvidberg.

Erklæring.

Da Ingen af alle de paa Regentsen boende Herrer Studentere har paa den fierneste Maade havt den allermindste Andeel i de her i Staden i de tvende Aftener, den 4de og 5te hujus, forefaldne Pøbeloptrin, erklærer jeg Den, som paastaaer det Modsatte, for En, der farer med aabenbar Usandhed.

Kiøbenhavn, den 6te September 1819.

R. Nyerup.
Provst paa Regentsen.

Kiøbenhavn, den 8de September.

Under 10de f. M. har det allernaadigst behaget Hs. Majestæt at udnævne kongelig fransk Statsminister, Marqvis Dessolle, til Ridder af Elefanten; samt under 1ste dennes, at benaade den danske Charge d'Affaires ved Hoffet i St. Petersborg, Kammerjunker v. Hennings, med Ridderkorset af Dannebrogordenens 4de Klasse.

Ifølge det kongelige danske Cancellies Skrivelse af 6te September til Hr. Saxtorph, som Decanus ved det kongelige Sundheds-Collegium, tilkiendegives samtlige her i Staden værende Læger, at de, saasnart de tage Nogen, der er blesseret, under Cuur, have indtil vidre uden mindste Ophold at give Politiet i Kiøbenhavn Underretning desangaaende.

Tirsdagen den 7de September 1819 ere i Tallotteriets 1143de Trækning i Kiøbenhavn følgende Nummere udkomne:

56. 57. 9. 12. 32.

Postefterretninger.

(Af Hamb. Corresp., Børsenhalle, allg. Zeitung og Altonaer Mercur.)

London, den 24de August.

I Løverdags, den 21de, holdtes her i Kron- og Anker-

Fig. 2. *Dagen*. 8th September 1819

Fædrelandet.

1850.

Abonnementspris i Kjøbenhavn 15 Mk. pr. Qvartal, 5 Mk. pr. Maaned, enkelte Nr. 6 Sk.; udenfor Kjøbenhavn 3 Rbd. pr. Qvartal frit i Huset. Hver Søgne-Aften udgaaer et Numer. Bladets Contoir, store Kjøbmagergade Nr. 54, er aabent om Formiddagen Kl. 11—1.

11te Aarg. **Mandagen den 29. Juli.** **Nr. 173.**

Foreløbig Rapport om Slaget ved Idsted den 25de Juli 1850.

I Henhold til de trufne Dispositioner rykkede den 2den Divisions 2 Brigader den 25de Juli Kl. 1½ om Morgenen frem fra Havetoft; den 5te Brigade rykkede Kl. 4 frem fra Helligbæk. Den sidste Brigade kom strax i Engagement og begyndte Kampen, der snart udviklede sig i en betydeligere Grad i vor høire Flanke, imod hvilken Fjenden foretog en omgaaende Bevægelse. Nogle Batailloner af 1ste Division sendtes her Fjenden imøde og tilbageviste Angrebet paa dette Punkt.

Veiret var meget ugunstigt med stærk Regn og Taage, saa at Intet i større Afstand kunde observeres. Der hørtes intet Engagement i østlig Retning, og ingen Melding modtoges fra anden Division.

Under disse Omstændigheder, da Oplysninger maatte indhentes ved udsendte Officierer og Ordonnanser, beordredes 5te Brigade til ikke at gaae længere frem, men at holde Kampen staaende, og hertil fremsendtes Understøttelse fra Reserveartilleriet. Nogen Tid efter erfaredes, at den Del af 2den Division, der efter Dispositionen skulde dirigeres over Øvre-Stolk, i denne By, efterat flere Batailloner vare marcherede derigjennem, samt i det Øieblik, at 13de Bataillon var omtrent midt i Byen, pludselig blev angreben ved morderisk Ild fra Husene. De fremgaaede Afdelinger bleve strax kaldte tilbage, og af de Insurgenter (over 1000 Mand) der tilligemed en Del Bønder havde udført dette Overfald, tilintetgjordes Størstedelen. Imidlertid vare af de høiere Officierer, som strax ilede til, Flere blevne enten dræbte eller saarede. Faldne ved denne Leilighed ere desværre Generalmajor Schleppegrell, Obersterne Trepka og Læssøe, Capt. Kranold; saaret Oberstlieutenant Bülow; samtlige blandt Armeens mest begavede Officierer.

Det kunde ikke være Andet, end at et saa pludseligt Tab blandt de Høistcommanderende og deres Stabschefer maatte fremkalde en Standsning og nogen Forvirring i Bevægelserne. Herpaa blev imidlertid snart raadet Bod. Generalmajor de Meza afsendtes med en paa Valpladsen dannet Stab, for at overtage Commandoen ved anden Division. Kl. 8 afgik Generalen hertil; men allerede tidligere vare 3 Batailloner af 4de Brigade under Oberst Thestrup afsendte, for at forene sig med den hos Oberst Baggesen værende Styrke. Kl. 9½ meldte Generalmajor de Meza, at han var beredt til at rykke frem. Da imidlertid de tidligere i den høire Flanke frempousserede Batailloner endnu ikke vare vendte tilbage, blev det bestemt, at Forceringen af Passene skulde udsættes en Time, efter hvilken Tids Forløb der paa hele Linien med Kraft skulde rykkes frem.

Den 3die Brigade var imidlertid Kl. 3 rykket frem imod Sollbro, og havde, skjønt først efter Fægtning og efterat have slaaet Bro under Fjendens Ild, forceret Overgangen. Fjenden kastedes derefter rask henimod Jübek, hvorefter Brigaden over Silberstedt Kl. 11½ ankom foran Schuby, der blev beskudt.

Kl. 10½ rykkede Armeens Hovedstyrke frem, for med stormende Haand at tiltvinge sig Gjennemgangen ved de forskandsede Passer mellem Arnholzsø og Langsø.

Efter en heftig Artillerikamp udførtes dette ved at 4 af den 6te Brigades Batailloner, iblandt hvilke Livgarden tilfods, under Oberst Irminger, sendtes frem, for i Forening med Oberst Ræders Brigade at forcere Passerne paa den vestlige Side af den mellem de nævnte Søer værende mindre Sø, medens en Del af 4de Brigade tjente som Reserve paa dette Sted, og medens Generalmajor de Meza med den tilbageværende Del af 2den Brigade og noget over 3 Batailloner af 4de Brigade som Reserve kastede sig paa den østlige Side af den nævnte lille Sø.

Ved dette Angreb brødes den haardnakkede Modstand, som hidtil havde stillet sig imod Indtrængelsen i Skoven foran disse Passer, en Modstand, der forøgedes ved det paa Siderne af Veien ufremkommelige Terrain, som forvandlede disse til lange Defileer. For Reservecavalleriet, der var trukken til Hovedcorpset, var derfor endnu ingen Anvendelse.

Den 1ste Brigade havde imidlertid været detacheret imod Wedelspang, uden dog at skulle forcere dette Pas; den havde 2 Batailloner i Øvre-Stolk og Resten henimod Wedelspang.

Den 3die Brigades Opgave, der saaledes var fuldstændig løst af Oberst Schepelern, og hvis Ankomst til Schuby saa fuldkomment coinciderede med Hovedstyrkens Fremtrængen over Passerne, bidrog ikke lidet til at Forskandsningerne hurtigere forlodes af Fjenden. Den Ordre, der under de tidligere ugunstigere Omstændigheder var afsendt til Brigaden, og som, formedelst den besværlige Communication over det ofte inpassable Terrain, først da modtoges, forhindrede imidlertid, at Brigadens Bevægelse, ved at fortsættes i østlig Retning, gav et endnu større Resultat.

Ved Sammenstødspunktet af Chausseen og den gamle Landevei og i Høide dermed paa Veien til St. Jürgen pousseredes nu Hovedstyrken rask frem; her detacheredes Reservecavalleriet mod Lyrskov og Schuby, for at rense disse Punkter, hvilket effectueredes ved Hjælp af Batteriet Wegener.

4de og 6te Brigade dirigeredes derimod mod Schuby, medens den øvrige Del af Hovedstyrken indtog en Stilling paa Høiderne Norden for Slesvig.

Efter at have afsøgt Skovene vest for Slesvig rykkedes dernæst omtrent Kl. 8½ Aften gjennem Byen til en Bivouakstilling fra Haddeby Noor bag Dannevirke henimod Schuby.

3die Brigade bivouakerede ved Neukrug som Reserve.

Denne Stilling var indtagen Kl. 12 Midnat, og først da etableredes Hovedqvarteret i Slesvig, som var besat af en Bataillon.

Fjenden menes at være gaaet tilbage med sin Hovedstyrke til Rendsborg og med een Brigade til Eckernförde.

Hans Tab har været betydeligt. Over 1000 Fanger ere indbragte. 2 Kanoner af Batteriet Baggesen, som bleve tagne ved Overfaldet i Øvre-Stolk, ere tilbageerobrede, desuden 5 Stkr. Skyts fratagne Fjenden. Paa Slesvigs Lazareth befinde sig omtrent 2000 saarede Insurgenter. Desuden blev en stor Del af Bagholdet i Øvre-Stolk tilintetgjort og det meste af Byen afbrændt. Mange døde Fjender henligge endnu paa Markerne, da man her ikke forefandt en eneste Vogn.

Vor Seir har styrket det moralske Element hos Soldaten, saa at han med ufortrøden Udholdenhed har baaret de Savn og udholdt de mageløse Anstrængelser, han i den sidste Tid har været underkastet. Den fortrinligste Disciplin har været herskende, og ingen Excesser ere komne til Overcommandoens Kundskab.

Men vi beklage Tabet af mange og dyre Offre. Overfaldet kostede os flere af vore udmærkede Officierer, og i det Hele have vi i det mindste 12 døde og 73 saarede Officierer, 104 døde og 2300 saarede Underofficierer og Menige.

Ikke desto mindre er Armeen fuldkommen kampdygtig.

Saadant er i det Væsenlige Grundtrækkene af en Kamp mellem to Armeer, der af Naturen og Forholdenes Udvikling ere bestemte til at virke i Forening.

Dagsbefaling.

Hovedqvarteret Slesvig den 26de Juli 1850.

Soldater! I have igaar retfærdiggjort mine Forventninger.

Efter en anstrængt March og efter at have kæmpet Dagen iforveien, under Savn af Ro og Hvile, have I beseiret en kraftig Modstand og kastet Fjenden ud af hans faste Stilling tilbage over Slien.

Soldater! Atter staae I paa det gamle Dannevirke.

Men nye Kampe, nye Anstrængelser vente Eder! I ville bestaae og udholde disse med samme Aand og Kraft som hidtil!

En mønsterværdig Disciplin og Orden har fundet Sted ved Besættelsen af Slesvig; jeg haaber, at den fremdeles vil blive iagttagen af Eder.

Soldater, jeg takker Eder!

Krogh.

David Copperfield juniors Levnet og Eventyr.

—

Sexogfyrgetyvende Capitel.

(Sluttet.)

Miss Dartle saae paa mig, som om hun vilde spørge, om der ellers var Noget, jeg kunde ønske at vide, og da der netop faldt mig Noget ind, svarede jeg:

„Jeg kunde ønske at erfare af denne — Karl", jeg kunde ikke formaae mig selv til at betjene mig af et forsonligere Udtryk, „om man har opsnappet et Brev, der blev skrevet til hende hjemmefra, eller om han troer, at hun har faaet det."

Han forblev taus og rolig, fæstede sine Øine paa Jorden og balancerede nøiagtigt Spidsen af hver eneste Finger paa sin høire Haand mod Spidsen af hver eneste Finger paa sin venstre.

Miss Dartle dreiede haanligt Hovedet hen mod ham.

„Undskyld, Miss", sagde han, vaagnende af sin Aandsfraværelse, „men hvor underdanig jeg end er imod Dem, saa kjender jeg dog min Stilling, skjønt jeg kun er et Tjenestetyende. Mr. Copperfield og De, Miss, ere to forskjellige Personer. Ønsker Mr. Copperfield at erfare Noget af mig, maa jeg tillade mig at erindre Mr. Copperfield om, at han kan gjøre mig et Spørgsmaal. Jeg maa holde over min Værdighed."

Efter en øieblikkelig Kamp med mig selv, vendte jeg mit Blik om imod ham og sagde: „De har hørt mit Spørgsmaal. Betragt det som henvendt til Dem, hvis De vil. Hvad svarer De?"

„Sir", sagde han, idet han snart adskilte og snart atter forenede Fingerspidserne, „mit Svar maa være betinget, da der er Forskjel paa at røbe det, Mr. James har betroet mig, til hans Moder og at røbe det til Dem. Jeg anseer det ikke for sandsynligt, at Mr. James kan have villet opmuntre Modtagelsen af Breve, der let kunde forøge en Misstemning; men videre tør jeg ikke tillade mig at gaae."

„Er det Alt?" spurgte Miss Dartle mig.

Jeg yttrede, at jeg ikke havde Mere at sige. „Undtagen", tilføiede jeg, da jeg saae ham fjerne sig, „at jeg fatter denne Karls Andel i den nedrige Historie, og at jeg, da jeg agter at underrette den brave Mand, der har været hende i Faders Sted fra hendes Barndom, derom, vil raade ham til ikke at vise sig altfor meget paa Gader og Stræder."

Han var bleven staaende, da jeg begyndte, og havde hørt efter med sin sædvanlige Rolighed.

„Mange Tak, Sir. Men De maa undskylde, Sir, at jeg siger, at der hverken gives Slaver eller Slavefogder her i Landet, og at Folk ikke have Lov til at tage sig selv tilrette. Gjøre de det, vil det snarere gaae ud over dem selv, end over Andre. Og derfor er jeg slet ikke bange for at vise mig hvor jeg lyster, Sir."

Med disse Ord bukkede han høfligt for mig og derpaa for Miss Dartle og gik sin Vei gjennem den buede Aabning i Christtorn Hækken, hvorigjennem han var kommen. Miss Dartle og jeg betragtede en liden Stund stiltiende hinanden, og hendes Væsen var ganske det samme, som da hun kaldte paa Karlen.

„Han siger desuden", bemærkede hun med en langsom Krusning paa Læben, „at hans Herre, efter hvad han har hørt, seiler langs med den spanske Kyst og naar han er færdig dermed fremdeles vil tilfredsstille sin Lyst til Sølivet, til han bliver kjed deraf. Dog dette kan ikke interessere Dem. Imellem disse to stolte Personer, Moderen og Sønnen, er Brudet blevet større end nogensinde, og der er kun lidet Haab om, at det vil blive lægt; thi de have eet Sind, og Tiden gjør dem kun begge mere halsstarrige og egensindige. Heller ikke dette kan interessere Dem, men det tjener til at indlede det, jeg har at sige. Den Djævel, De gjør til en Engel, jeg mener den simple Tøs, han trak op af Mudderet", vedblev hun, med sine sorte Øine fæstede paa mig og sine lidenskabelige Fingre rakte i Veiret, „lever maaskee — saadanne usle Kreaturer skulle jo være seiglivede. Er hun i Live, da er det Deres Ønske, at en saa uskatterlig Perle maa blive funden og tagen i Bevaring. Det ønske vi med, paa det at han ikke atter ved et eller andet Spil af Tilfældet skal blive et Bytte for hende. Forsaavidt ere vi forenede i een og samme Interesse, og derfor er det, at jeg, der kunde tilføie hende alt det Onde, en saadan gemen Skabning er i Stand til at føle, har ladet Dem kalde, for at De skulde erfare det, De har hørt."

Af Forandringen i hendes Ansigt saae jeg, at der nærmede sig Nogen bagved mig. Det var Mrs. Steerforth, der rakte mig Haanden med større Kulde, end fordum og med endnu større afmaalt Værdighed i sit Væsen, men tillige — jeg saae det og det rørte mig — med en uudslettelig Erindring om min fordums

— 689 —

Fig. 3. *Fædrelandet.* Monday, 29th July 1850: Three columns and the feuilleton novel: Chapter 46 of *David Copperfield*

Den til Forsendelse med de Kongelige Brevposter privilegerede
Berlingske politiske og Avertissements-Tidende.
№ 17. Tirsdagen den 21. Januar. 1873.

Fig. 4. *Berlingske politiske og Avertissements-Tidende.* 21st January 1873, front page

About the middle of the century some newspapers began to have three columns and to use the feuilleton and approximately at the same time the use of the bold print-type helped in dividing the long colums into more easily readable units (see figures 3-6).

Nicolai Haase, Pilestræde Nr. 11.

udsælger i denne Maaned Frynder, Agramaner og couleurte Besætningsbaand til nedsatte Priser.

Pengebesparelse.

Ludvig Holberg som Lærer i Historie.

Selverhverv,

Forskrifter

Bertran de Born.

Færskvandsfiskeriet.

Det mechaniske Misforhold

Robert af Normandiet

Nye Musikalier.

Robert af Normandiet,

Wilhelm Hansen,

Blandede Bekjendtgjørelser.

Beskæftigelse for Damer.

Original-Udgaven af Laurentius,

Herdahls Børne-Tidende,

Frits Jensens Frøhandel,

Hædersdiplom for Markfrø,

Youngs

Patent Paraffin-Olie, 1ste Sort,

Crystal Oil

samt

Youngs prima Paraffin-Lys,

Youngs Paraffin Light & Mineral Oil Comp., Limited.

Price List.

Rudolph Knudsen.

Carbolsæbe.

Carbolsæbe

Lægeattester:

Helsingørs Sæbefabrik, i Januar 1873.

Ægte amerikanske Regnfrakker

Pilestræde 45, 1ste Sal.

Nyeste Patent-Fodtøi,

Frimærkesamlere

Havanna-Cigarer.

Hvid Petroleum 18 ß

Gode, brugte Herreklæder

For Damer.

Anatherin-Mundvand

Billigt Postpapir.

44 ß.

C. M. Albeck,

Ledige Tjenester.

Volontair.

En Husjomfru

Tjenestesøgende.

Gartnerplads søges.

Et Par gifte Meierifolk,

Forvalterplads søges.

Avlsforvalter.

Forpagtning søges.

Et Meieri

Fig. 5. *Berlingske politiske og Avertissements-Tidende.* 21st January 1873, page 4

The provenance principle for telegram news, mostly in regard to foreign countries is predominant. For inland news we see the emergence of the single article with headlines in bold. The advertisements begin to abandon the gothic-type/black letter. They experiment, and the advertise-

Tillæg til den Berlingske politiske og Avertissements-Tidende.

№ 17. Tirsdagen den 21. Januar. 1873.

Henviisninger.

Dampskibsfarten i Sundet.

Kjøbenhavn-Malmö.

Til Lübeck

Ystad-Rønne.

Til Gøteborg

Mandariner

Kul.

Handelsefterretninger.

Telegrammer

Fig. 6. *Berlingske politiske og Avertissements-Tidende.* 21st January 1873, front page of supplement

ments very often cover two columns now, and still more progressive: at the top of a page they may even cover all the columns. Each advertisement is an isolated entity. The advertisements begin to disrupt the ribbon of text, they begin to invite the reader to read or perceive the texts in a differ-

Skanderborg Amts Avis
og
Avertissementstidende.

Nr. 235. Fredag den 9de Oktober 1885. 10de Aarg.

Fra Fortiden.

Benyt Øjeblikket.
Under Godtkjøbs-Udsalget sælges:
3 til 400 Al. heluld. hjemmev. Hvergarn,
2 - 300 - halvuld. do. do.,
1000 - hjemmevævet Tvistlærred.
Alt til virkelige Indkjøbspriser.
Wictor Wittrup.

Fig. 7. *Skanderborg Amts Avis.* 9th October 1885, front page

ent manner than the journalistic text: they do not invite a linear reading of the texts. On the contrary, each advertisement tries to attract the reader's perception and to divert it from the neighbouring advertisement!

Fig. 8. *Skanderborg Amts Avis.* 9th October 1885, page 2

Being a genuine provincial newspaper *Skanderborg Amts Avis* was not revolutionary in layout, but each article became independent by the use of blank space and headlines in bold. The advertisements (and the

Fig. 9. *Aarhus Amtstidende*. 6th June 1899, front page

title of the newspaper) were quite modern in their use of Latin characters (see figure 7).

By comparison page 2 is monstrous (see figure 8). It is totally filled with text, but even the use of blank space and headlines is not enough to create readability. It should be added that a newspaper like *Politiken*

Gratis Lysttur til Hamborg den 1ste April.

Klip hver Dag denne Del af Bladet med Dateringen ud! Se nærmere inde i Bladet!

Dagligt Oplag langt over 28,000.

Forposten

Læses daglig af Alle.

Redaktion: Kultorvet 3, 1ste Sal. Telefon 5720. Redaktionssekretær: Cand. phil. Wilh. Jensen.

Expedition: Kultorvet 3 Stuen. Telefon: 5720. Expeditionen aaben 9—7.

Nr. 842. | Hver Middag. | Udgiver og Redaktør: Johannes Hansen. | Onsdag 6. Februar. | 1901.

Modbydelig Sædelighedsskandale paa Øen St. Thomas.

Et mærkeligt Forhør og en mærkelig Retspraxis.

Svinerier mellem Mænd. — Læs Artiklen paa 2den Side.

Hotel „Bryderen".

Koks fra Københavns Gasværker.

Husholdningskul og Cokes

Falentin Drost & Jensen.

Stort Billard Gevinstspil.

Hotel „Blaagaard", Blaagaardsgade 13.

Cokes

Flindt, Drost & Co.,

„Alaska".

Frøken Otto.

Mohr's Margarine

Herregaardssmør

Damer og Kvinder.

100 Systuer til Dame-Linned

Tarliong & Co.

Klæde-Huset.

Krone-Brød

Karnevalet

Jydsk Forening

Even Neuhaus,

Proteinbrød.

Hofbager Olsens Søn.

20 Stk. Daadyr

Fasaner,

Sjællandske Kalkuner.

Java Caffe 98

En Sergent skudt sig paa „Tre Hjorte".

En offentlig Kvinde mishandler sig selv

Paagrebet.

Indbrudet i Mercurh-Cyklelageret.

Johannes Hansen.

Fig. 10. *Forposten.* 6th February 1901, front page

was organised in a similar way from its outset in 1884, but the use of larger headlines aroused the reader's interest. It was a broadsheet newspaper, it had a very distinct and clear layout and except for foreign news each article was distinct from the other.

By the end of the century it was possible for the newspapers to

Folkets Avis

Nr. 3843. | Udgaar hver Dag. | 2 Øre. | Redaktør: Emil Rex. | 2 Øre. | Onsdag 9. Septbr. | 1908.

Dansk Koloniallotteri.

4de Trækning 17de September.

Fornyelsen slutter paa Lørdag d. 12. Septbr.

Forhandlere af A. Formann & Co. Blodbudding

CHAPCHAL FRÈRES WERA № 90

Gehejmekonferensraad Alberti arresteret for Falsk og Bedrageri.

Den største Skandale i Verden.

Peter Adler Alberti.

Arbejdet standset i Malmøs Havn.

Den første Tilstaaelse.

Grundlovsforhøret

I Spjældet.

I Albertis Hjem.

Interview med Fru Alberti.

Fig. 11. *Folkets Avis.* 9th September 1908, front page

choose any format from the tabloid form to the 'blanket' form. They could cultivate the classic look with up to seven or even eight columns: a highly aesthetic and austere layout with all the problems of reading this implied: a linear reading of three broadsheet pages with very little space left for the eye to rest.

Fyens Stiftstidende

Oprettet ved kgl. Privilegium 1772

Adresse-, politisk og Avertissements-Avis

14lde Aargang. | Fredag den 20de September 1912. | Nr. 220. 12 Sider.

Freden.

Konstantinopel, Torsdag.

Ministerraadet behandlede i Dag Indberetningen fra de officiøse Fredsforhandlere; Ministerraadet kunde imidlertid ikke komme til nogen Afgørelse.

Efter dets Afslutning udtalte et Medlem af Kabinettet, at Italien hidtil ikke har nærmet sig de tyrkiske Forslag, og betonede, at Porten ikke vilde gaa ind paa noget Forslag om Erstatning.

Et Dementi.

Konstantinopel, Fredag.

Udenrigsministeriet dementerer Meddelelsen om, at Ministerraadet skulde have afbrudt Fredsforhandlingerne. Disse vedvarer tvertimod og er id en bedste Gænge. Ministerraadet vil sandsynligvis den 22. September træffe en afgørende Beslutning i Sagen.

En Vedtagelse.

Franske Arbejdere.

Le Hâvre, Torsdag.

Det almindelige Arbejderforbunds Kongres har vedtaget en Dagsorden, i hvilken Forbundet erklæres for fuldstændig uafhængigt af alle politiske Partier, og enhver politisk Virksomhed indenfor Fagforeningerne forbydes.

To Dueller og en Beskyldning

Budapest, Fredag.

Morgenbladene meddeler, at Spektaklerne i Deputeretkamret har givet Anledning til to Dueller. En Deputeret har beskyldt Ministerpræsidenten for at have begaaet Underslæb af Statens Midler til Beløb 4 Mill.

Skandinaviske Flyvninger

Fra København til Stockholm.

Stockholm, Torsdag.

I Følge „Dagens Nyheter" er det lykkedes at tilvejebringe det Beløb, der er fornødent for en Flyvning mellem København og Stockholm.

Præmien bliver i gunstigste Tilfælde 10,000 Kr., ved en mindre vellykket Flyvning 6000 Kr.

Der føres i Øjeblikket Forhandlinger om de nærmere Enkeltheder. Flyvningen kan ikke finde Sted før tidligst i næste Uge.

Hvis Forholdene bliver særlig gunstige, tror Flyveren Dahlbeck, at han kan udføre Flyvningen med kun een Mellemlanding i Jønkøping eller i Malmslätt.

Den sammenlagte Flyvetid vilde blive ca. 5 Timer. Flyvekonkurrencen vil blive international.

Stockholm—Gøteborgflyvningen opgivet.

Stockholm, Torsdag.

Den paatænkte Flyvning mellem Stockholm og Gøteborg, som skulde være begyndt i Morges, er bleven opgivet.

Saavel Kaptajn Sundstedt som hans Maskine var Kl. 9 klare til Start, men Aëroplanets Ejere forbød Starten, da de ikke vilde riskere Maskinen for en saa vanskelig Fart.

Eksplosion.

Konstantinopel, Fredag.

Ved en Bombeeksplosion i Moskeen i Aritschebi i Vilajetet Adrianopel er der dræbt 50 Mennesker og saaret 120.

Dræbt og plyndret af sin Broder.

Et Jernbanedrama.

(Privat for „Fyens Stiftstidende").

Berlin, Torsdag.

Mellem to smaa Stationer i Nærheden af Saarbrücken er en Passager i Iltoget bleven dræbt og udplyndret. Ved Stationen Busendorf blev der trukken i Nødbremsen, og Toget standsede straks, hvorefter 3 Mand sprang ud og tog Flugten. Den ene blev straks greben.

Man fandt saa i den Kupé, hvorfra de var sprungen ud, Liget af en Mandsperson med Knivstik i Hoved og Bryst. Det viste sig, at den fangne Gerningsmand var den Dræbtes *egen Broder*.

Efter al Sandsynlighed er det lykkedes den Myrdede under Kampen at trække i Nødbremsen.

Afbrudt.

(Privat for „Fyens Stiftstidende").

London, Torsdag.

De engelske Manøvrer er i Aftes pludselig bleven afbrudte. Det har hidtil været umuligt at opspore Grunden til denne mærkelige Foranstaltning, der overalt har vakt Forbavselse.

Nyt Badehotel paa Thurø.

Et stort, moderne Hotel.

* *Svendborg*, Fredag.

Det naturskønne Thurø har navnlig i de senere Aar været stærkt søgt af Turister, og mange Sommergæster har for kortere eller længere Tid slaaet sig ned paa den smukke Ø for at søge Hvile og Rekreation.

Man har dog i nogen Grad savnet et Badehotel, idet den iøvrigt fortræffelige Kro med tilhørende Sommerpensionat selvfølgelig kun kunde modtage et begrænset Antal Gæster. Mange har derfor maattet leje sig ind hos Private.

Nu har et stedligt Konsortium, repræsenteret ved Gdr. *P. Andersen*, Gambetgaard, af Skibsbygmester *Tolstrup* for 4000 Kr. købt en 4 Tdr. Land stor Grund paa „Grønne Odde", hvor det er Hensigten at opføre et stort, moderne Badehotel med Plads til 60—70 Gæster.

Det nye Badehotel, der ventes opført næste Foraar, vil faa en herlig Beliggenhed lige ved Svendborg Sund og i de mest idylliske Omgivelser.

Konsortiet, der ogsaa sørger for bekvem Dampskibsforbindelse med Svendborg, har endvidere af Kaptajn *Martin Rasmussen* købt en nærliggende Ejendom for 5000 Kr., som man vil indrette til Brug for Badehotellet, hvis Pladsen i dette skulde blive for knap.

Luftskibsbesøget i København.

Zeppelineren lander paa Flyvepladsen.

Om Zeppelinluftskibets Ankomst til København i Gaar bragte vi jo allerede i Gaar et længere Privattelegram fra vor Korrespondent, som imidlertid i Dag sender os endnu nogle smaa Enkeltheder fra Landingen.

„En af Tilskuerne", skriver han, „løftede en sød lille 6 Aars Pige op, og under Leveraad fra de omkringstaaende overrakte hun Greven en Buket — hendes Haand var den første, der bød Luftens Konge velkommen.

Toldvæsenets Eftersyn var snart forbi — der var virkelig en Toldassistent sendt ud for at inspicere ved Ankomsten.

En Repræsentant for vort Blad fik Posten til vore Abonnenter udleveret.

Vi talte med en af Passagererne. „Det var en herlig Tur", siger han. „Rolig og støt gled vi hen over Land og Vand. Temperaturen var behagelig, og Skibet gik saa støt, at jeg under Turen kunde barbere mig selv. Luftsyge var der ikke noget, der hed, og alle var vi lige glade over Turen.""

„Hansa" passerede paa Hjemvejen Lybæk Kl. 3½ i Gaar Eftermiddags og naaede ved 4-Tiden Hamborg, hvor det foretog flere Flyvninger over Byen, hilst med Begejstring af uhyre Menneskemængder, der havde samlet sig paa de aabne Pladser, paa Hustagene og overalt, hvor Luftskibet kunde sés.

Kl. 4½ gik „Hansa" videre til Luftskibshallen, hvor det landede glat Kl. 4,40.

Saaledes endte det første Luftskibsbesøg i Danmark efter at have faaet et ualmindelig heldigt Forløb.

Gondolen med Grev Zeppelin nærmer sig dansk Jord paa Flyvepladsen i København.

En Automobilulykke under „Hansa"s Besøg.

København, Torsdag.

Paa Amager Boulevard skete der i Middags en uhyggelig Automobilulykke.

Folk kom gaaende i store Skarer fra Flyvepladsen efter at have set „Hansa", da en Bil pludselig kørte ind paa Gangstien. Det var nødtvungent, at den gjorde det. En Cyklist drejede nemlig pludselig foran den, og for at undgaa at køre ham ned, drejede Chaufføren brat til Side og fo'r ind paa Gangstien, som var aldeles fyldt med Mennesker, der forfærdet flygtede til alle Sider. En ung Dame, Frk. Olivia Weikop, der spadserede med sin Forlovede under Armen, blev revet ind under Vognen, hvis Hjul tog fat i hendes ene Ben, der blev frygtelig læderet, saa Benstumperne stak frem to Steder. Endvidere forslog hun Hovedet slemt imod Stenbroen. Cyklisten, en Kontorassistent Charles Krüger, som var den egentlige Aarsag til Ulykken, blev slynget ind paa Fortovet, hvorved han paadrog sig endel Kvæstelser.

Ambulancen og Redningskorpset blev tilkaldt, og medens Redningskorpset bragte Damen til Rigshospitalet, blev Krüger kørt til Sundby Hospital og efter at være forbundet her til sit Hjem.

Chaufføren, som vistnok har kørt for stærkt, er foreløbig suspenderet fra sin Stilling.

Mod Tyrkiet.

Et Treforbund.

(Privat for „Fyens Stiftstidende".)

Berlin, Torsdag.

Fra Wien meldes fra paalidelig Kilde, at et Forbund mellem Bulgarien, Serbien og Grækenland mod Tyrkiet nu er en Kendsgerning. Det er Forbundets Hensigt at foretage en Aktion mod Tyrkiet.

Dagens Ulykker.

Dræbt i en Motor.

Holeby, Torsdag.

Sognefoged P. Olsen, Holeby, er i Gaar kommen ulykkelig af Dage.

Han var beskæftiget med sin Motor og kom derved for nær til Remtrækket, blev grebet af dette og fik Hovedet knust; han døde paa Stedet. Der var ingen til Stede, da Ulykken skete.

Den Forulykkede var 45 Aar gl.

Falden af en Vogn og dræbt.

Frederikshavn, Torsdag.

Gaardmand Julius Hansen, Mosen i Hørby, faldt i Gaar ned af en belæsset Vogn og paadrog sig saa alvorlige Beskadigelser, at han i Morges uden at være kommen til Bevidsthed afgik ved Døden.

Styrtet ud af et Vindue og dræbt.

Aalborg, Torsdag.

I Gaar Eftermiddags styrtede en 3½ Aar gammel Dreng, Søn af Murer Petersen, Slotsgade i Aalborg, ud af et Vindue og forslog sig saa slemt, at han nu er død.

Fyrsteligt Bryllup

Wien, Torsdag.

I Slotskirken i Wallsee er i Formiddags Erkehertuginde Elisabeth Franziska bleven viet til Grev Georg af Waldburg-Zeil. Højtideligheden overværedes af Kejserfamilien med Kejser Franz Joseph i Spidsen.

Den strandede Motorbaad.

Hillerød, Torsdag.

Den ved Liseleje strandede Motorbaad hedder „Inga" og er, efter hvad der er oplyst, i Mandags stjaalet fra Hellerup Havn. Den tilhører Overretssagfører Dyrhauge.

Den ligger nu i Hundested Havn.

En Herregaard i Flammer.

Aalborg, Torsdag.

I Eftermiddag Kl. 5 opstod Ild i Hovedgaarden „Dybvadgaard" ved, at en Motor eksploderede i Laden.

Ilden bredte sig med voldsom Fart, Laden og Kostalden er nedbrændt. En Del Kalve og Svin er indebrændt.

Man frygter for, at saa godt som hele den store, gamle Herregaard vil brænde.

(Senere Telegram).

Laden var fyldt med Korn.

Man mener nu at kunne redde Hovedbygningen og Hestestalden, der er teglækket.

„Dybvadgaard" ejes af Godsejer Winkel, Hillerød.

„Arbejde adler" i Nyborg.

Konsul Thuesen udtaler sig om den nye Forenings Arbejde og Planer.

* *Nyborg*, Fredag.

Siden Bestyrelsesvalget i Foraaret i Landsforeningen „Arbejde adler" har man ikke hørt ret meget til Foreningens Virksomhed, og vi har derfor nu spurgt Udvalgets Formand, Konsul *Thuesen*, om, hvorledes Bestyrelsens Arbejde havde formet sig.

Konsulen svarede:

„Vi har ikke ligget paa den lade Side, men har i den forløbne Tid gjort alt muligt for at skaffe en egnet Ejendom med Lokaler til Oprettelse af et Arbejderherberg her i Byen.

Forholdene har imidlertid i saa Henseende været meget ugunstige, da alt i denne Sommer har været optaget af Militæret; men til Foraaret bliver der jo sikkert Plads nok, og vi har da ogsaa Tilbud paa Lokaler til den Tid.

Udvalget har i Sommer beset forskellige Arbejderherberger paa Fyen og i Jylland og sat sig ind i Driften af disse.

Naar Herberget her i Nyborg er oprettet, vil der blive oprettet et mellem Nyborg og Svendborg, og det er da Tanken at udsende Skiltene til Medlemmerne."

Konsulen beder os ved Samtalens Slutning opfordre vore Læsere støtte Sagen ved at melde sig ind i Foreningen, da Køb af Lokaler til Herberget og Bolig til Værten vil tage mange Penge.

Indmeldelser modtages af Konsul *Thuesen* (Telefon 40) og Bankdirektør *Dahlerup* (Telefon 243).

Fig. 12. *Fyens Stiftstidende.* 20th September 1912, front page

Otherwise they could continue in the direction that had been initiated by the ads: larger headlines, which covered several columns. They began to relinquish the linear reading model and began the construction of the topographical layout with multi-layer headlines.

It can be seen from figure 9 that *Aarhus Amtstidende* has the classical look, but that this look is killed by the advertisements, which constitute the only place where the eyes can rest! However, the most important article is distinguishable: The fifty years of the constitution (Grundlovsjubilæet).

Forposten was the most outstanding example of the popular press ('skandalepressen') (see figure 10). The articles are easily distinguished from each other: the titles or headlines use Latin characters (of different fonts!), there are headlines covering the whole page but referring to an article on page 2. Even more remarkable, the multi-layer was common at the turn of the century; here you have one covering six columns. We have all the elements needed for 'modern' newspaper layout.

And finally, the newspapers, in a larger covering headline, present individual articles (sometimes with their own heading), which can cover several columns (see figures 11 and 12).

The newspapers become a kind of topographical display. They have abandoned the linear ribbon-strip text. The reader can skip articles; he/she can jump from one article to another. The headlines are guiding tools. The use of multi-deck headlines creates islands where you get the central information and can set out to get more details – if you wish to.

In the 1940s the topographical system is well established. It still remains the principle today, perhaps tabloids being the only exception. They do not have any front-page text and normally use titles and headlines to announce what is inside, as did *Forposten* with its headline covering six columns.

The single news item cannot be a completely independent unit until the newspaper has used a topographical headline design. Also the isolation of each news item – the specific identity of the news item – is a prerequisite for changing into a construction of relevance. The inverted pyramid and the use of instalments are only possible if the article has both a frontier at the beginning as well as one at the end!

	Number of newspapers	Number of articles
1870–1879	11	288
1880–1889	14	488
1890–1899	11	327
1900–1909	20	848
1910–1914	07	343

Table 1. The number of newspapers investigated

The investigation of news in 63 newspapers

This article is based on the systematic reading of 63 newspapers covering the years 1873–1914, with one additional newspaper from 1927, and taking into account articles from newspapers in the period 1940–1942. Table 1 contains a global list indicating for each decade the number of newspapers and the number of articles in these newspapers (for more details see Appendix 1).

Reading and counting news articles was systematic, but it cannot be said that the choice of newspapers was systematic. For a representative sampling, a good corpus should be based on the same number of newspapers from each period; provincial papers and papers from Copenhagen, papers from the bigger provincial towns and from the smaller ones, right-wing papers and left-wing papers, popular papers and serious papers, etc. Obviously, some 63 papers – unequally distributed – could never meet this standard, especially when there should be newspapers from every year. If, however, we had chosen the papers with an interval of 5 years we could have risked seeing ruptures where there were none!

Imperfect as it is, the sample is useful anyway. It helps to ask the right questions, it helps us to get an idea about the general movement, and it is a useful tool to construct purely qualitative analyses of news texts.

All the articles have been registered in a few categories: News, reports from meetings, comments, short news/notices and Other – a category that covers reports, features, all kinds of fiction and cultural stuff that does not have the aspect of news. Much news is presented in

	News articles		Reports of meetings	
	In numbers	In percent	In numbers	In percent
	lin int rel	lin int rel	lin int rel	lin int rel
1870–74	22 – 00 – 00	100 – 00 – 00	17 – 00 – 00	100 – 00 – 00
1875–79	43 – 01 – 02	93 – 02 – 04	13 – 00 – 00	100 – 00 – 00
1880–84	16 – 00 – 00	100 – 00 – 00		
1885–90	63 – 06 – 32	62 – 06 – 32	23 – 00– 04	85 – 00 –15
1890–94	13 – 00 – 03	81 – 00 – 19		
1895–99	21 – 06 – 14	51 – 15 – 34	21 – 00 – 00	100 – 00 – 00
1900–04	41 – 10 – 32	49 – 12 – 39	02 – 00 – 00	100 – 00 – 00
1905–09	54 – 16 – 29	55 – 16 – 29	20 – 00 – 05	80 – 00 – 20
1910–15	24 – 21 – 22	36 – 31 – 33	17 – 00 – 04	81 – 00 – 19

Table 2. Repartition of structures of the articles

notices, but any notice that is so short that it is reduced to a piece of information like this one: 'X arrived yesterday at Y' has been relegated to the category of 'notices', they are too short to show either a linear structure or a relevance structure or to have the aspect of a narrative. As for the distinction between the linear articles, the articles showing a relevance structure and the intermediate forms, I have to admit that this distinction is a very problematic one. When is an intermediate structure no more intermediate, but a relevance structure?

Table 2 contains the repartition of the three categories for news articles (soft and hard news) and for reports of meetings for each of the nine five-year periods, first in number of articles, then the repartition in percentage of the news articles in the three categories: linear (lin), intermediate (int) and relevance structure (rel).

Even if these figures lack statistical significance they show nevertheless that we move from a state of total linearity to a more complex situation, where the linearity begins to fade out. In fact the numbers for linear structures cover the examples of narrative constructions, but no attempt has been made to count the narrative structures, the numbers being too small and the distinction between genuine linearity and narrative structures being too complex and uncertain. On the other hand, a counting based on two unstable categories, simple linearity and narrative linearity, would suffer from having extremely low reliability.

One thing seems obvious; reports from meetings did not change at the same speed and rate as 'proper news' articles. While attempts were made to change this dinosaur of Danish journalism - the thorough, detailed and boring reports of meetings - the changes seem to have been structurally uneasy (see the paragraph 'The changing of reports of meetings' below). In the following decades the detailed reporting of meetings died out.

Linear and non-linear principles in newspaper articles

Découper dans la réalité – to cut in reality

The journalistic reconstruction of reality requires tools, conceptual tools, cognitive frameworks, structural models. How has it come that journalistic ideology talks about the editorial 'news tools' as if these tools were simply 'transport devices'? The famous WH-questions that in journalistic ideology are the warrants of neutrality and objectivity are such models. The WH-questions are routines, are tools (cf. Mouillaud & Tétu 1989, 16).

There is no mass newspaper without journalistic models and routines. A newspaper must have models that can create order on the page - out of the disorder of the world.

But what were these models to capture in order to tell events? How were the models created? How did they tell the events? How do they tell the events today?

The story line and the discourse line

From the very beginning of the existence of newspapers, until about 1880, the linear representation is the way to capture events. The discourse line matched the story line (cf. Chatman 1978, 63ff.).

This construction principle works well if the subject matter (the story) is simple, that is, if the evolution of events can be contained within one temporal line. If the event is complex and has several lines, actions with temporal ramifications going on at the same time, the linear model is problematic. The reports in the Danish press about the French Revolution 12th-15th July 1789, or the terrible Battle of Isted in 1850, are good illustrations (for the problems of temporal ramification, see Øhrstrøm 1998, 253ff.).

But as long as the story line is simple, a similar discourse line is a perfect way of presenting (reconstructing) events. Two examples:

1) In the year 1885 cabinet-makers and joiners began to organise their trade unions in the provinces. Two members of the Board of the trade union in Copenhagen visited 13 towns within 18 days. On 9th June 1885, *Social-Demokraten* wrote a rather long article of 80 lines about this event (=campaign). The article strictly follows events in the last five of these towns on a day-by-day basis, giving a resume of each meeting as close to the chronological story order as possible. Here is the end of the article: 'Berg and Jensen arrived at Copenhagen after a journey of 18 days, having been to meetings in...'. Then the 13 towns in chronological order are listed. The article may seem a bit bewildering for a modern reader, but it is easy to understand, and with a bit of training you will find this way of presentation perfectly normal!
2) On 9th October some farms in the district of Skanderborg were put on auction. As a political action directed against the Conservative Government, the owners of these farms had refused to pay taxes. The political party to which the farmers belonged, the Peasants Party, had accused the Conservatives of using illegal ways of preparing the budget. The auction therefore was a highly political action (I shall not, however, go into further details about the parliamentary debates of the late 19th century in Denmark). The whole article covering this event is linear, the selling of each object is described in a linear order; the different incidents are presented in a linear way. This is marked by the use of temporal indications or indications of succession: 'At twelve o'clock', 'next object', 'a bit later', 'after that', 'then', 'next object', 'suddenly', 'it went on like that for a quarter of an hour', 'then', 'once again', 'next object', 'then once again', 'suddenly', 'some time afterwards', 'still', 'at two o'clock', etc.

Such linear texts are easy to read, but they present some problems:

a) They invite the reader to read the whole text; often you have to reach the last piece of information in the text to understand what it is about. In the case of the two trade union organisers we must read that they have now returned home or something similar in order to conclude the text. In the inverted pyramid, however, one can gain from the headlines or lead an idea about the closure, an idea about the end of the story line. In that way it is not necessary to go to the end of the discourse line to get the end of the story line. Not so in the linear discourses!
b) As long as the newspapers had only two or three small pages of reading stuff (tabloid or a format between tabloid and broadsheet) the linearity was no problem; the model reader and the actual reader is someone who has the time to read. But if the reader (actual or model) has less time, or if the newspapers become bigger, it is not sure that the reader can read the whole paper!

The Skanderborg story is more complicated, we know that there were incidents going on at the same time, so we therefore have the feeling that we are not given the full story. Articles like the Skanderborg story seem to rattle off information, there is nothing to indicate what is important and what is less important – the reader is lost when he/she has to read long articles. News reports with a structure like the Skanderborg story may be easy to read, but they are difficult to grasp. And are they easy to remember?

The temptation of narrativisation
Much news stuff can be turned into a narrative according to this model:

– Initial situation (orientation)
– Establishment of conflict
– Actions
– Solution/non-solution
– final situation
– eventually, the moral of the story

This model is the basic narrative scheme according to the Swiss text linguist Jean-Michel Adam (cf. Adam. 1992, 54–58). Allan Bell uses the Labov model for personal narratives to get a model that seemingly is valuable for the structure of news in newspapers: abstract, orientation, complicated action, evaluation, resolution, coda (cf. Bell 1991, 148ff.; cf. Labov 1972, 354 ff.). Bell misunderstands the model when he even makes it a model for newspaper stories; he has to discard the temporal problem and the problem of the withholding of information. But he stresses nevertheless the fact that there are similarities also. The important thing is that there is a rupture, a complication, and that a solution is found to this complication (*denouement* in dramaturgy). The narrative first gives us the clue for understanding at the end. Only at the end do we realise that the pattern of causality has determined the evolution. This is what Gérard Genette calls 'retroactive determination' (cf. Adam 1992, 54).

These models seem to be 'universal'. Branigan presents a similar model saying that 'Nearly all researchers agree that a narrative schema has the following format...' (cf. Branigan 1992, 14).

Here are some examples of the use of narrative devices:

On 9th June 1885, *Social-Demokraten* makes a report about the way the newspaper's sub-editor (Wiinblad) had been taken to court over an article he had written earlier about military affairs. In his report of 9th June 1885, Wiinblad makes a satirical portrait of his opponent and presents himself as a poor, innocent and inoffensive person. He plays with different points of view, indicates clearly the strong points of the evolution (complicated action and referring to the absence of solution), and all of these literary devices give the text a strong ironical character.

The same year, 1885, a young man made an attempt on the life of the conservative (and dictatorial) Prime Minister Estrup. On the 22nd October, *Sorø Amtstidende* (liberal opposition) made a report, here reduced to a resume of the main points:

1) The rumours in Copenhagen presented with a dramatic *mise en scene*.
2) The rumours were right.
3) The scene of the attempted murder:
   – Estrup has just come home; he is outside the front of his house.
   – Young man suddenly turns up and shoots.

– Estrup: 'Do you want to kill me?'
– Young man shoots once more.
– People arrive to rescue Estrup.
– The front door is opened from inside.
– Estrup goes in.

4) He has not been hurt.
5) Estrup: 'Well now I can say that someone has tried to kill me'.

The whole story has an implicit narrator who points out (indirectly) how the different actions should be understood, and finally the Prime Minister closes the incident with a kind of moral.

Such narratives are mostly to be found in everyday stories. One type of story was very much used by the popular press; i.e., reports from court. On the whole, short stories about people who had been sentenced to smaller fines, or humoristic stories with very strong emphasis on the narrator or the point of views. In the 24th July 1889 edition of the popular *Aftenbladet* there are 10 of these stories! The stories have a common headline 'From the police court', with the single story having no headline, but the first line has an indentation, and the names of the protagonists are marked with spaced letters. Each story is thus clearly distinct from the others. Here is a translation of one of the stories:

The sun was shining, the birds were singing and the hip-flask [in Danish, *lommelærke* = pocket lark] was singing in the pocket of the servant Adolf Zøllner. To have something solid to eat with the brandy, he bought a smoked herring from the fishmonger Ana Olsen. As it happened, Miss Olson's boyfriend arrived at exactly the same moment. Zøllner gave him a swig from the bottle, but this did not please 'the lady'. She struck out against the bottle and cried out to her boyfriend: 'you stupid idiot, are you going to drink with that pig?' - After that Zøllner punched the lady in the face. The price of the herring and the brandy was three crowns.

The narrative has the advantage of presenting a good story, it is easy to understand, important elements and less important elements are easy to distinguish, and it is easy to remember (cf. Branigan quoted above). The reader is captivated. But the narrative solution has its disadvantages too.

In a good story you withhold information (cf. Bordwell & Thompson, 482; Branigan 1992, 66), there is a constant play based on the disparities of knowledge, you only realise the pattern of causality at the end (the retroactive determination). As we have seen this is one of the fundamentals in story telling. But serious information in newspapers is not a play or a game. The journalist has to deliver the information as quickly and as 'willingly' as possible. He/she should not play with the reader, as does the author or the film director. If he does so, the focus is on the text – on the fascination of the text (as in the reports from the court!) and not on the referent. Talking with Roman Jakobson we could say that news stories are focused on the referential function, not on the poetic function.

Narratives are normally marked by the existence of a narrative voice, a point of view, a level from which the story is told, a narrator. This, however, is a bad device in news reporting. In the emerging journalistic ideology, news is not told by someone – it is not submitted to a point of view – news is there, the facts are there, the press just collects them!

Narrativisation means also that the story becomes more or less self-contained, as Harms Larsen puts it: 'In fiction, *deixis* is only valuable within the limits of the story' (cf. Larsen 1991, 150). If the news story is told according to these lines it begins to look like fiction. But news is not fiction; news is fact. A self-contained *deixis* cuts the links to our actual world. And news must have a clear link to actual reality. That is the fundamental contract. And this contract is very strong when the information is important – especially if we are dealing with political information. The way stories from the police court are told in *Aftenbladet* makes them look like fiction – but this has no consequences for credibility: these reports are by nature pure entertainment or fun.

As mentioned before it is very often difficult to distinguish linear, chronological description from true narratives. The narrative solution existed since the very beginning of the printing press (the casual leaflets). It seems to have been rather widely used in the period 1880-1910, but it was probably never predominant. It was mostly used in stories where one person opposed the other, in crime stories or humorist stories from everyday life, but was normally absent in political affairs. However, the impact of narrativisation varies much over time. In the 1940s the narrative structure seems to have been rare, while today it seems rather acceptable, at least in the popular press. I am convinced that the period 1885–1895 was the golden age of narrativisation, here even political stuff seems to rely heavily on it, as well as fictionalisation. I am not in favour of linking a long-term evolution, i.e., the changing of news structure, to the history of events. But the (still hypothetical) extraordinary use of narratives in the period 1885–1895 could very well be due to the fact that direct reporting of political affairs was dangerous and that the literary devices were an easy cover up. Narrativisation was a useful procedural tool in the very harsh political climate of that decade.

We can now conclude the following:

The narrative structure has always been a possibility and was used to a greater or lesser degree according to the journalistic ideals/ideology in vogue at the time, and probably also according to the political climate. In the long run narrativisation was not the solution, as journalism became a matter for professionals of a specific kind and the literary devices were assigned to a more humble place.

Today you will find that most narratives are located in a specific place in the news story: the linear main event. For some researchers this is a pity! The linear construction (narrative or simple chronological/spatial linearity) had some cognitive advantages and it had high entertainment value. According to Lewis, news items (Lewis talks about television news) constructed with narrative structures are easier to retain and much less boring than the ordinary news items in a news bulletin (cf. Lewis 1994, 25ff.). If we follow Lewis, it should be clear that the narrative structure was assigned to a minor role in newspaper stories, not because of its (lack of) inherent values, but because it did not cope with the overload of information that became a problem at the turn of the century.

The principle of relevance

Thus the narrative solution was not the general solution, it remained, and remains, a secondary one. It did not reduce the time spent by the reader. It only imperfectly facilitated his/her comprehension of the text. The solution was the inverted pyramid, the principle of relevance described by van Dijk in several of his articles from the 80s. In a very rough way the new system can be described as follows:

1) The most important elements of news or an abstract of the news comes first.
2) The same element of information can be repeated several times, but normally in more detail, with different focus and with decreasing importance (instalment principle).

The ultimate consequence of this structure was that the withholding of narrative information became impossible. A change of such importance took about 40 years, but the linear story coexisted for a long time with texts using the relevance principle. On the 5th June 1911 the newspaper *Riget* relates the death of a young recruit. The story is completely linear; there are only few narrative devices in spite of the fact that the content strongly invites narrative. The headlines make a very short resume of the story; the rest is linear. Even in 1911 the evolution towards new structures was far from being accomplished - and *Riget* was not a somnolent provincial newspaper!

The relevance structure can be described in many ways and textbooks on journalism have different ways of describing it. Here I follow van Dijk in *News as Discourse* where he too has different ways of presenting the structure (van Dijk 1988, 52-57).

Here are the van Dijk news schema categories, but put into a linear chronological order:

R (resume), Hist (history), Pre (previous events), Cir (circumstances), ME (main event), Con (consequences), Com (comments).

This presentation is of course not without problems, Cir does not necessarily come before ME, and Com and Con are not related in time to each other, etc. But it is rather close to the linear presentation in the newspapers 1875–1910. This linear presentation stressed the Pre and ME, with some use of His and Cir. Com was not an isolated category, there were comments scattered all over the text, comments were integrated - in general.

1: Total linearity
Hist - Pre - (Cir) - ME - Con - (Com).

2: The main event ME is in the headlines and within its place in the story.
R (=ME1) Hist - Pre - (Cir) - ME2 - Con - (Com).

3: ME is in headlines, beginning and middle! But still with some linearity.
R (=ME1), ME2 - Hist - Pre - (Cir) - ME3 - Con - (Com).

4: The consequences move in front of the text.
R (=ME1/Con), Con - ME2 - Hist - Pre - (Cir) - ME3 - Con - (Com).

5: The temporal order has vanished or it has been inverted in the discourse line.

The five stages are purely hypothetical and prototypical, and may even be slightly anachronistic. The evolution did not follow specific models: the category 'circumstances' was not used very much. The newspapers before World War I did not give many explanations, they took it for granted that the reader agreed with the opinion of the paper (the political party press) and also that he/she had, to some extent, the knowledge necessary for understanding. At any rate the final result as we see it today is that the discourse line differs fundamentally from the story line. The temporal progression of the discourse line is totally inverted, but we can normally reconstruct some kind of story line, the succession of events.

How this inversion of order has been established is still not fully explored. The change is not only an issue of media research; it is an issue of cognitive psychology (according to van Dijk) and of narratology. We may gain some hopes from the research of Keisuke Ohtsuka and William Brewer, even though they are - unfortunately - more occupied with oral narratives. We need to improve our knowledge of journalists' own descriptions of the phenomenon: when does the new structure become a normative and conscious model for the work of journalists? Presumably the changes did not begin as a part of a conscious project; the first changes were imperceptible.

But we can point out the conditions necessary for the structural change and we can line up some types of (news) stories/informative texts where the relevance principle could be readily at hand as a model.

– The individualisation – in some way or another – of the piece of information is a precondition.
– The oral narratives introduced by an abstract, an argument for telling the story (cf. Labov 1972, 363-64).
– The influence from descriptive non-chronological texts: portraits, obituary texts.
– Reports of debates on bills and other law propositions: the bill has been presented and approved (event); then follow explanations and details about the new law – and even references to the debates. These texts are a blend of chronological structures and a-chronological descriptions.
– The crime story, the trial. Main event: the murder, the corpse. Then we follow the detective line, we find the murderer and finally we are told what happened before the murder. But this story could just as well be told from the very beginning: events preceding the murder, then the murder, etc. So in the case of the crime stories we have two possible structures: a simple chronological story about the successive events or the stressing of the main event, the murder, the point from which the rest is told.
– The influence of the telegrams from the news agencies. This may be true – but the telegrams reproduced by the newspapers investigated in this chapter do not confirm this hypothesis.

In most textbooks you find two explanations as to why the discourse order in journalistic texts is very different from the story order:

The inverted structure enables the reader to choose whether he/she wishes to read the whole article or should be content to read only the resume – and it enables the (sub-)editor to cut the end section off articles which are too long – the main information will still be there.

This final stage is a well-established and conscious routine or device. The intermediate stages would normally not allow cutting at the end. To which extent were these stages conscious? In 1885 no journalist could imagine or foresee how the news structure would be in 1915! For years, even though some important information was placed at the beginning, the articles still kept important information till the end of the story.

Here are some examples of intermediate constructions of the news story:

Politiken, 12th June 1885:

Story 1

Headlines:	Olaf Poulsen in Bergen [OP was a famous Danish actor].
Lead:	Private telegram from Bergen: The performance of OP Wednesday was a great success.
Context:	The comedies performed.
Main info:	A linear resume of how OP acted, and the public's reception.

Story 2

Headlines:	Man shoots himself.
Main event:	Man shot himself at a public baths (identification details).
Cont.+cons.:	Assistant sees man and does not suspect him, hears shot, finds the dead man, corpse deposited in the office.

Both (short) pieces of news do not have a completely linear structure. In the first story we get the important information three times: OP is in Bergen (= is performing at the theatre). In the second story the death is important (we get this information twice), but as there is no further information about the dead person, the perspective changes and we follow the assistant from his point zero: the arrival of the candidate for suicide.

The two following stories have come closer to the inverted pyramid:

Kolding Folkeblad, 18th of June 1885:

Story 3

Headlines:	No headlines: only use of bold for the first five words.
Main event:	Supreme Court has made a decision in an administrative trial (not indicated which decision).
Consequence:	A decision that probably will be tried at the Supreme Court.

History:	The churchwarden has asked to be paid for ringing the church bells at the burial of the late Queen (four years ago). Payment refused by the governing church council. A detailed description of the reasons follows.
Main event:	Supreme Court has decided that the parish must pay.

Story 4

Headlines:	No headlines: only use of bold for the first three words that in fact function as a headline. Resume: Abominable crime on a British ship.
Main event:	Details about how the Swedish sailor was killed – and the captain's defence.
Main event:	Death of the sailor after incredible suffering.
Consequence:	The captain tries to cover up the story.

Story three is interesting in that it is moving towards a relevance structure, but tries to keep the old structure even with some true narrative devices (the withholding of information): First we get the information that the Supreme Court has made a decision, then a linear history and finally we get the content of the decision.

Story four is the crime story which takes place at sea – seen from land: We learn about the death and then we move to the beginning, the persecutions which the sailor underwent, we follow the evolution and end up with the first consequences of the crime.

The four stories show – if this should at all be necessary – that from the simple linearity to the relevance structure the intermediate nuances are numerous. And they might suggest that the crime story is an ancestor of the relevance story: main event first then the explanation.

On 24th July 1889 *Aftenbladet* has a story about abused children (even then!):

Headline: The word 'Monster', which is at the same time an evaluation. Then the main event follows (the verdict), then history/context, then events preceding the trial, and finally the happy consequences: the child is liberated.

The crime stories (crimes, verdicts) were an experimental field, where new routines and models were tried. The crime story is equally suited to narrative structures as well as to relevance structures.

But we should not consider this evolution towards the inverted structure as something like a smooth and equal movement towards a well-defined goal. We may feel that the popular press was in many respects the press that pushed this movement. While this may be true, even this press showed strange divergences. On 6th February 1901, *Folkets Avis* and *Forposten* bring the same story about the suicide of a staff sergeant at an inn in Copenhagen.

Folkets Avis relates the main event, the suicide, four times within an article of 70 lines:

Headlines:	The killing
Lead 1:	The killing
Lead 2:	Arrival of the staff sergeant – and his death
Main event:	Detailed report of events from the beginning (1 a.m. until he was found dead (description): now there is a change of viewpoint, we see the sergeant's death through the eyes of the landlord.
Consequence:	Police arrive.
Comments:	Information about the sergeant.

Forposten makes a much shorter article, half the size of *Folkets Avis*.

Headlines:	The killing
Main event:	Report of events from the beginning until he was found dead (description): there is no change of viewpoint, from the very beginning we see the sergeant through the eyes of the landlord or the personnel.
Consequence:	Police arrive.

The first article has a structure not far removed from what you find in popular newspapers today or even in the quality morning papers that normally present the main information twice (or more) in the beginning and then return to the main event in a linear narrative. *Forposten* has a much more classical structure: a very short headline, plus the rest in totally linear order.

About 1910 or slightly afterwards, the news stories, especially the political stories, are more and more organised according to the relevance principle. Just one example:

In 1908 Alberti, the Minister of Justice, was arrested for fraud. The amount of money involved was enormous. The scandal was enormous. *Folkets Avis* wrote an article covering three columns with headlines equally covering three columns: something quite exceptional for this period.

Headlines:	Alberti arrested.
Lead:	The official announcement functions as lead: Alberti arrested.
Main event:	Alberti arrested (linear description, narrative).
History + previous events:	Causes for his arrest.

The rest of the article consists of new information that has turned up, of reportage and an interview with Alberti's wife.

The problem for *Folkets Avis* (and for the other newspapers!) is clearly the overload of important information. Any futile detail becomes important in this context. The newspaper has only one way to cope with the situation: to keep adding the incoming information as it arrives! In fact the relevance principle has already given us the main information, the incoming information needs no further explanation. The relevance principle is much more efficient in such context than the narrative or the linear discourses. This is equally clear if we look at the way the murder of the Austrian archduke Franz Ferdinand is treated in the liberal provincial *Østsjællands Folkeblad* from the 30th June 1914. The killing is repeated at least four times in the beginning and then new information is added as it arrives.

The inverted structure never really became the only solution, even if the newspapers around 1940 had very few articles with narrative or other quasi-linear structures. The inverted structure was adopted for its practical usefulness: it was easy for production purposes; it was easy for the reader's orientation. But it was not a good solution for comprehension and memorisation! In this regard the inversion of the temporal order, the cutting and the splitting of the events was not a good solution. According to Ohtsuka and Brewer three principles are at stake when we understand and remember texts. These principles facilitate our comprehension and memory:

1) *The immediate integration principle*: The new element or event can be related directly to the events already mentioned in the text.
2) *The consistency principle*: There is an underlying frame or mental model that new elements or events fit into.
3) *The isomorphism principle:* The succession of events or the succession of spatial details is followed in the text (the linear principle).

The inverted structure does not follow 3, it may not follow 1, and as for 2 it is more uncertain how this principle and the inverted structure fit together (cf. Ohtsuka & Brewer, 322-23). But in spite of these principles, that no one was conscious of, the inverted structure became the model for the news story.

The changing of reports of meetings

The reports of meetings, especially the parliamentary sessions, were extremely important. They were not as numerous as the news stories, but the reports were long, and they were considered important. Reports from Parliament in the 19th century were normally placed on page one and covered the first column(s). They were the linear texts *par excellence*. However, in the 63 newspapers studied, slow and rather timid changes only occur after 1900, which is more than 15 (20?) years later than the news stories.

In 1906 *Berlingske Tidende* still wrote reports of less important meetings in the classical linear way, but the more important and long reports began with a resume, an explanation of what was important – in fact a resume and a comment. While this was not very clear in the report of the parliamentary session, it was clear in the report of the meeting of the Copenhagen City Council on 23rd January 1906. The report begins with general information about the debate, then a block of five resumes of the five items/issues of the agenda.

The administrative structure of Øresund Hospital.
The administrative personnel of Copenhagen City Hospital.
The health insurance of gas workers.
The regulations covering pubs in Copenhagen.
The suppression of a tramway line.

For each issue there is a resume of seven to 18 lines. Finally there are the reports of the debates covering each of these issues. The reports of each issue vary from 24 to 32 lines with smaller characters than the resumes, thus indicating that the resumes inform, but that you can get more if you are willing to tire your eyes! Although it is rather mechanical, the structure of the article shows that the newspapers are perfectly aware that the reader does not necessarily read the whole article. It should be added that at the beginning of the 1900s, there were very few news articles, but a lot of notices and background material. A report about the politico-military relations between France and Venezuela was as linear as the articles from the 1880s. This is a rather strange constellation, because normally the linear principle was abandoned in the news articles before it was in the reports!

Epilogue

By 1940 the relevance principle became *the* principle. Almost every article about events was presented according to this principle, even stories that could have been narratives like the court reports. On 17th August 1940, *B.T.* (one of the few popular papers remaining today) relates an assault on an innocent holiday visitor. Twenty lines plus headlines is not a long article, but we are given the main event - the assault - four times at the beginning, and then the consequences! And on 21st May 1941, *Aftenbladet* relates a railway accident with headlines about the consequences of the accident, the whole article being a constant shift from consequences to main event and back again. It is not until the end of the article that we are given information about the beginning of the accident. You really have to look thoroughly to find narratives in 1940–1942.

In the period 1915–1940 changes were accomplished. I have examined one newspaper (!) from the twenties in more detail: *Viborg Stiftstidende* from the 17th of August has eight political news stories all with the inverted structure. The paper has 25 non-political stories (soft news and crime): 12 are linear (and narrative), 11 still show an intermediate structure and only two have the inverted structure. This is of course anecdotal, but it fits very well with the hypothesis that the inverted structure was a way of signalling that the information was serious. And political events are serious. The necessity of being serious is the only reason why even small stories like the assault on an innocent holiday visitor were told with the inverted structure. The 1940 story is dull and it is boring. The journalists from the popular papers around the turn of the century could have made a fascinating story out of this stuff.

The inverted structure has become an ideological signal: truth and serious information even in the most trivial affairs. The inverted structure has thus three functions: It facilitates the production, it reduces the reading time, it appears as a warrant for serious information, but as we have seen, it is not sure that it facilitates comprehension and memorisation.

As mentioned before, newspapers today have not abolished the narrative solution, the popular papers (and even the serious) may still tell the main event as a linear narrative and you can still find small narratives about trivial affairs. Here is a story, which appeared in *Jyllands-Posten* on 23rd January 1999, about the cutting of four lime trees:

Headlines:	Lime trees cut down when the owner was on holiday.
Man returns from holiday:	His trees have gone!
Next day:	Search to find the guilty party.
	Local administration is guilty.
The local administration:	The trees (on municipal ground) were too old.
Man:	Some of them were on my ground (proof).
The local administration:	You are right, this is a bad story. Plant new trees?
Man:	I want my trees back.

The article withholds information: We learn who is guilty at the same time as the protagonist.

The story begins 'in medias res' with the discovery of the missing trees, follows the conflict, the administration proposes to solve the problem but the man refuses, because there is no solution. There is a shift in viewpoint from the man to the administration and vice versa. The elements are there; the non-solution at the referential level is a solution (*dénouement*) at the story level. Such stories can easily be constructed; they have great entertainment value, as had the police court reports a hundred years ago. They are easy to understand, it is easy to identify with the protagonist and it is easy to remember the story. But such stories are not exactly common.

Finally it should be noted that the news story of today is slightly different, the van Dijk categories of verbal reactions, expectations and evaluations have gained more importance. The information (main event) comes increasingly from interviews with the main actors and is presented through interviews. This evolution can be explained by the convergence of at least three factors:

1) In the old political press journalists and public shared a common culture and knowledge, not a very extended one, but sufficient to understand events and texts. Today the complexity of information is overwhelming. Too many journalists are specialists in nothing except writing. Thus they have taken up the habit of asking experts and they (the journalists) share no knowledge with the readers who are supposed to know nothing. In this case the use of interviews is a solution for the journalist – and for the reader.
2) The strong emphasis in journalism is on neutrality. Both sides should have the chance to express themselves (objectivity). They are therefore represented in the news text. The journalist is less responsible.
3) The possible influence of television. The information has become a montage of pieces of interviews, and the like, as on television.

Conclusions

This article is a plaidoyer for a long and medium-term media history. A history that follows the dying forms as well as the emerging ones. Normally when you read history, especially media history, it is a history of the forms and the concepts that had won. They are the goal of history to historians. When *Politiken* had been modernised in 1905, history had come to its term and the evolution of the more conservative newspapers was without interest. That the old formats continued for more than two decades in parts of the country is of no interest. And if it is difficult to establish when a movement begins, it is even more difficult to say when it stopped.

It is a *plaidoyer* for a history that does not focus on the importance of a single person or group of persons: a history that gets rid of the Cavling fascination (and the short-term history).

It is a *plaidoyer* for a history that sees the ruptures not as ruptures but as the consequence of a long movement that has finally been realised by the social actors. In fact the structure of news is the expression of working routines, and working routines change slowly, imperceptibly, but at a given moment they become conscious, and that is the change.

It is finally a *plaidoyer* against a widespread belief that today everything goes faster and faster. We should not forget that our social environment also consists of elements or compartments where things change slowly; they are stable as compared to other compartments. We should also remember that in some compartments speed has changed. I would claim that the newspaper structure changed - if not rapidly at least fundamentally - from 1800 to 1900/1910, and that in the 20th century the newspaper structure has been extraordinarily stable.

We still need a more thorough and long-term investigation of the mediacy problem: What is specific for each media and how is the media configuration established each time a new media comes up? How does a new media influence the old media internally and how is a new media influenced by the old? (cf. Niels Brüggers text in this volume). How important was the impact of the advertisement in the changing of news pages in the second half of the 19th century? Has the newspaper at all been influenced by radio? Has it been influenced by television?

References

Adam, Jean-Michel 1992. *Les textes: Types et prototypes*. Paris: Nathan.

Bell, Allan 1990. *The Language of News Media*. Oxford: Basil Blackwell.

Bordwell, David & Kristin Thompson 1990. *Film Art: An Introduction*. New York: Mc Graw-Hill.

Branigan, Edward 1992. *Narrative Comprehension of Film*. London and New York: Routledge.

Braudel, Fernand 1996(1969). *Ecrits sur l'histoire*. Paris: Flammarion

Chatman, Seymour 1978. *Story and Discourse*. Ithaca and London: Cornell University Press.

Drotner, Kirsten et al. 1996. *Medier og Kultur*. Copenhagen: Borgen.

Febvre, Lucien 1968(1942). *Le problème de l'incroyance au 16ème siécle*. Paris: Albin Michel.

Jamet, Claude & Anne-Marie Jannet 1999a. *La mise en scène de l'information*. Paris: L'Harmattan.

Jamet, Claude & Anne-Marie Jannet 1999b. *Les stratégies de l'information*. Paris: L'Harmattan.

Jensen, Jens F. 1998. *Multimedier, Hypermedier, Interaktive Medier*. Aalborg: Aalborg Universitetsforlag.

Labov, William 1972. *Language in the inner City*. Philadelphia: University of Pennsylvania Press.

Larsen, Peter Harms 1990. *Faktion som udtryksmiddel*. København: Amanda.

Ledin, Per 1995. *Arbeternas er denna tidning*. Stockholm: Almqvist och Wiksell.

Lehrmann, Ulrik 1999. Skandaleblade, skillingsviser og smudsblade. Ib Poulsen & Henrik Søndergaard (eds.), *Mediebilleder*. København: Borgen.

Lewis, Justin 1994. The absence of narrative. *Journal of Narrative and Life History* 4(1-2), 25-40.

Meilby, Mogens 1996. *Journalistikkens grundtrin*. Århus: Ajour.

Mouillaud, Maurice & Jean-François Tétu 1989. *Le journal quotidien*. Lyon: Presses Universitaires de Lyon.

Ohtsuka, Keisuke & William F. Brewer 1992. Discourse Organization in the Comprehension of Temporal order in Narrative Texts. *Discourse Processes* 15, 317-36.

Søllinge, Jette D. & Niels Thomsen 1989. *De danske aviser 1634-1989*, vol. 2 (1848-1917). København: Dagspressens fond/Odense Universitetsforlag.

van Dijk, Teun A. 1988. *News as Discourse*. Hillsdale, New Jersey: Lawrence Erlbaum.

Øhrstrøm, Peter 1998. Multimediernes tid. Jens F. Jensen, *Multimedier, Hypermedier, Interaktive Medier*. Aalborg: Aalborg Universitetsforlag.

Appendix 1

Newspapers, sorted by date

1873
Berlingske Tidende, 21/1.
Aarhuus Stiftstidende, 21/1.
Aarhus Amtstidende, 21/1.
Socialisten, 7/8.
Fædrelandet, 9/8.

1875
Aftenposten, 23/1.

1877
Horsens Folkeblad, 4/1.
Horsens Folkeblad, 8/1.
Jyllandsposten, 23/1.
Horsens Folkeblad, 23/1.

1879
Fædrelandet, 22/12.

1883
Nationaltidende, 18/2.

1884
Politiken, 4/10.

1885
Morgenbladet, 5/6.
Social-Demokraten, 9/6.
Politiken, 12/6.
Kolding Folkeblad, 18/6.
Skanderborg Avis, 9/10.
Sorø Amtstidende, 22/10.
Politiken, 28/10.
Politiken, 3/11.

1886
Morgenbladet, 7/2.
Hobro dagblad, 19/4.
Frederikshavns Avis, 8/9.

1889
Aftenbladet, 24/7.

1890
Aftenbladet, 6/1.
Aalborg Amtstidende, 18/12.

1894
Østsjællands Folkeblad, 9/8.

1896
Aftenposten, 16/4.

1898
Aftenbladet, 12/7.
Demokraten, 27/12.

1899
Aarhus Amtstidende, 1/6.
Aarhus Amtstidende, 6/6.
Aarhus Amtstidende, 2/9.
Demokraten, 5/9.
Politiken, 31/12.

1900
Forposten, 11/2.

1901
Forposten, 6/2
Folkets Avis, 6/2.
Aalborg Amtstidende, 26/7.
Aftenbladet, 8/1.

1903
Middagsposten, 4/1.
Odense Avis, 8/1.
Aftenbladet, 8/1.
Klokken 12, 8/1.
Aarhus Posten, 8/1.

1904
Ekstrabladet, 12/2.

1906
Jyllands.Posten, 23/1.
Aarhuus Stiftstidende, 23/1.
Berlingske Tidende, 23/1.
Aarhuus Stiftstidende, 30/1.
Social-Demokraten, 31/1.
Pressen, 24/7.

1908
Demokraten, 7/1.
Folkets Avis, 9/9.

1909
Dagens Nyheder, 5/9.

1911
Riget, 5/6.

1912
Fyens Stiftstidende, 8/3.
Riget, 20/4.
Fyens Stiftstidende, 20/9.

1914
Østsjællands Folkeblad, 30/6.
Østsjællands Folkeblad, extra, 3/8.
Hovedstaden, 4/8.

1927
Viborg Stiftstidende, 17/8.

When the 'Wireless' Became Radio

Carin Åberg

We often seem to confuse a technology of distribution with what is distributed by the technology, calling both 'a medium'. When we look at radio from a historical point of view the technology of distribution becomes a distinct criteria, while radio as a medium today is more often referred to as a certain area of content and forms, i.e. programmes. Making this distinction, questions of radio's 'mediacy', the medium in its specific way of being – its actuality and potentiality; the dialectics between contemporary ideas and material restrictions; and the configuration of mediacy at a certain point in time – become important features in understanding the creation of radio as a mass medium.[1]

In this essay, I will sketch the development of two 'radio genres' or programme types – one probably originating with radio and one adapting already existing forms of mediation to the specifics of radio as consisting solely of sound. By accounting for the status of, and debate around radio drama and 'DJ music shows' at different points in time, as well as their relationship to other public forms of mediated content, this will also constitute an example of the development of a technology of distribution – the wireless – becoming the distinct 'medium' of radio.[2]

1. For the concept of 'mediacy', see Niels Brügger's essay 'Theoretical reflections on Media and Media History' in this volume.
2. This essay draws on findings within a project accounting for the general development of production techniques and practices in Swedish radio and television between 1925 and 1985. The project is mainly based on publications made by radio professionals, annual reports and internal archive material from the Swedish Public Service Company, *Sveriges Radio* (see Åberg 1999a). It is furthermore part of a nation-wide project of writing the history of the public service era in Sweden – *De svenska etermediernas historia* [The history of broadcast media in Sweden]. Some additions also come from my Ph.D. thesis (see Åberg 1999b).

Radio: Content and technology

Radio today is said to be facing major changes, mainly due to the development of digital technology. Nevertheless, it is striking how the current development in the field of electromagnetic distribution – digitalisation – seems to be reminiscent of the development of the application of electricity during the late half of the 19th century. The common feature is the application of new technologies to already existing events in society, creating new combinations, integrating former distinct features and functions, thus creating a number of specific new media. During the turn of the 19th century and the following decades, film became a social institution and the essential theoretical solutions for wireless broadcasting of sound and images had emerged. However, neither the media of film, radio nor television existed as the media we know of today. Instead a complex of different – but already occurring – forms of performances were distributed by means of wires as well as without them, by celluloid tapes, metal wires and metal cylinders. Inscribed in the socio-cultural and politico-economical development the new mass media emerged (Flichy 1995). Today the implementation of the Eureka-147 project[3] ('DAB') around the world suggests the birth of a new medium – a wireless transmission of an integrated complex of images, texts and sound, albeit still called radio (Åberg 1999c).

Radio is recognisable as a set of programmes covering topics such as news, sports and current affairs, but also containing music, reading aloud of short stories and novels, and occasionally providing performances of poetry and drama. Generally speaking radio is mass distribution of information and amusement. However, radio is also a technology for distribution – the wireless transmission of sound. The content transmitted by this wireless technique is nevertheless also distributed in other forms – news, sports and current affairs on television and in newspapers; novels and short stories in books and weekly magazines; music on CD's, records and cassette tapes; drama and poetry on stage and television, and in print. The most specific feature in this

3. The technical project initiated by EU for developing digital wireless distribution of sound, images and text (see, for instance, www.worlddab.org/).

case, delimiting radio from other forms of distribution, is that radio is sound - speech and music - organised into distinct, but from time to time changing, forms of expression.

A brief background: Telecommunication, mass distribution and the private sphere

Counting the birth of radio as a medium from the innovation of the triode, or as is usually done, from the date of the first successful experiment of telecommunication employing electromagnetic waves propagated through space, misses the events by which the wireless became radio. Radio *waves* are used not only in radio broadcasting but also in wireless telegraphy, modern telephone transmission, television, radar, navigational systems, and space communication, just to mention a few applications. The ideas forming radio as a mass medium can hardly be found in wireless technology, but in the social, cultural and legal implementation of it.

Wireless technique also becoming broadcast radio was not a self-evident fact, neither was the idea of a distribution directly into people's homes. The first attempts to distribute sounds and voices from one point - the actual live event - to several distant receivers, a dispersed audience, by means of electricity were certainly not by way of a 'wireless' but a 'wired' medium: the telephone. During some years at the very beginning of the 20th century, in Paris, telephone owners could subscribe to mass-distributed theatrical performances from, for instance, the *Paris Opera* by a device presented at the World Exhibition in 1881, the *Théâtrophone*. Later on in London the same idea, now called *Electrophone*, was introduced expanding programming to also include sports results, church services and vau-de-ville. However, already in 1883, probably building on the idea of the *Théâtrophone*, a kind of 'sounding newspaper' - *Telefon Hírmondó* - was introduced in Budapest. By 1889 over 6,000 subscribers could get time signals, news, weather and financial reports as well as concerts and official statements distributed by telephone (Briggs 1985, Hinnen 1987, Löfgren 1990). However, according to Patrice Flichy (1995), the conception of the telephone did not from the beginning include private use, it was an improvement of the telegraph and to be used mainly for the telecommunication of commercial matters.

This seems also to be the main understanding of wireless telecommunication at that time – it was an issue most of all for military or business point-to-point two-way communication. Thus the first systematic use of radio communication comprises naval navigation and wireless telegraphy. The idea of using the new innovations of both radio and telephone in the field of public distribution with the receiver located inside the home seemed strange and was opposed and contested:

> When the Marconi company began broadcasting in 1920, there were complaints that this use for entertainment of what was primarily a commercial and transport-control medium was frivolous and dangerous, and there was even a temporary ban, under pressure from radio-telephonic interests and Armed Forces. (Williams 1975/1990, 32)

The 'inappropriateness' of using the new innovations of distribution for other purposes than commercial or other kinds of 'serious' telecommunicative necessities also concerned the phonograph: installations of a 'phonographic juke-box' in public places in the US were for some time determinedly opposed by the patent holder himself, Thomas Edison (Flichy 1995, 65).

However, combinations of different contemporary ideas merging one-way 'mass' distribution of live performances, commercialism and wireless transmission, occurred. In Sweden, for instance, a hotel owner installed microphones and loudspeakers in both of his two hotels. By means of the telephone net he could use the performance of one orchestra in one hotel and transmit the music to the other, thus getting musical entertainment in both of his hotels. This 'closed-circuit' distribution became mass distribution when the local amateur radio association tapped his wire and broadcasted the music wirelessly (*Falu rundradio fem år*).[4]

Thus, what later on became typical 'radio programmes': opera and concerts as well as popular music of the time, news, stock market updates, weather forecasts and sermons, were during this time publicly distributed in several ways. Out of this emerged three public media – film, radio and television, and at least one private – the telephone;

4. The number of receivers at the time is unknown.

socio-cultural institutions with characteristics of their own, features such as areas of content and forms of expression as well as their appropriate use.

At the time of the institutionalisation of 'radio' in Sweden in 1925, at least one thing was settled: it was a wireless distribution of programmes from one point (the public service company) directly into the homes of the Swedish population.

Wirelessly transmitted live events

Raymond Williams, writing on technology and cultural form in television, claims that as far as broadcast media is concerned, the technology of distribution comes first, while content counts as a secondary and less important issue. This remark seems quite accurate with regard to the Swedish history of radio and the establishing of the public service radio company - *Radiotjänst* - in 1925. In the debates preceding the founding of the company almost nothing is said, besides not allowing commercials, about what to distribute by this new technique (Elegemyr 1984). Looking at the programming during the first years of the Swedish broadcasting company, a considerable amount of time is devoted to music - concerts, opera, musicals, performances of dance music from restaurants, etc. Besides this, drama, poetry, lectures, the reading aloud of novels and short stories, reports from sports events, sermons, chronicles, weather and financial reports, news reviews and very early (in 1928) educational programmes produced for use in public schools, can be found.[5] As may be noticed several of the words I use are generic ones, and they are all to be found in the programming sheets of the time. This clearly points to the fact that the content of radio at that time, the 'programmes' were most of all distributions of

5. As was the case in several other European countries, the new radio company was not allowed to have a news-gathering service of its own. In Sweden the press owned half of the stock market shares of the radio company *Radiotjänst*, a fact that probably put restrictions on the company's news service. Furthermore, the first managing director of *Radiotjänst* also was the managing director of a national newspaper agency *Tidningarnas Telegrambyrå* (Elgemyr 1996).

forms of expression prevalent in society, originating from the public sphere: performances of music, drama, lectures, sermons etc; and forms of social gathering in bourgeoisie homes: reading aloud and intimate musical entertainment. The only real production of radio programmes inside the radio company can be found in the organisation and reading of news reviews, chronicles, different kinds of reports, etc. – re-mediations of content found in other media of the time.

How these genres came to be radio programmes no one really knows, but the experiments with electrical distribution, accounted for above, were probably a main source of inspiration. Another prominent factor was probably the very idea of radio as the 'wireless', denoting a large-scale distribution of events, far beyond anything physically possible in the past, and possibly making events otherwise limited to a small-scale audience accessible on a world-wide scale.[6] Several of the things appearing as programmes consisted of this kind of distribution of otherwise public events, facilitated solely by the use of a microphone, an amplifier and a wireless transmitter. In Sweden the broadcasting of live musical events was the preferred and most frequently used type of programme. To start with, these musical programmes were performed in a public place and transmitted further by radio, but after a short time they took place inside the studio itself. Statistics based on programming sheets show that radio output already from the inception of the public service company in Sweden consisted to a large extent of music (see table 1).

The total output of music time has since then been between 40 and 60%. However, a radical change occurred in music categories during the 1950s when popular music reached a top place at the expense of classical music. Generally speaking the output of music between 1950 and 1985 consisted mainly of popular music (over 50%) and only 33% classical music (Schyller 1996).[7]

6. The similarities with the promotion of the Internet today are striking (see Spinelli 1996).
7. Schyller's study covers every fifth year 1925–1990, but includes also the year 1994. The figures for 1990 and 1994 indicate that the total output consisted of equal amounts of classical and popular music.

The four top programme categories every fifth year 1925–1940			
Year	Category	Percent of total programming time	Total share of programme categories (%)
1925			51
	Classical music genres	36	
	Public messages	13	
	Popular music genres	11	
	Facts	10	
1930			44
	Classical music genres	19	
	Mixed music genres	15	
	Facts	13	
	Popular music genres	10	
1935			49
	Classical music genres	20	
	Mixed music genres	18	
	Popular music genres	11	
	Facts	10	
1940			41
	Classical music genres	19	
	Mixed music genres	14	
	Facts	9	
	News	9	

Table 1. The four top programme categories according to share of total programming time (Schyller 1996, 88)

Radio drama on the other hand, also appearing during the very first years, and although controversial and respected, has never had a large share of programming time. During the periods measured by Ingela Schyller it never exceeds 5% of total programming time, and since 1965 the share of radio drama is constant – 1% (Schyller 1996, 14).

Problems with music on record

Both live and recorded music formed part of the very first attempts at wirelessly transmitting of sounds. For instance, the experiments made by Lee de Forrest[8] contained music in the form of opera arias. Moreover, in the literature on radio history, David Sarnoff's statement on making radio a 'household utility' is frequent, and taking for granted that the content of radio is preferably music – radio as a 'music box' (Flichy 1995, Matelski 1993). Music also proved to be the most commercially successful type of radio content, above all in the U.S. And as indicated above, it also constituted the preferred output in the content-regulated public service radio company in Sweden, *Radiotjänst*. Furthermore, in Sweden, as well as in other countries, music was wirelessly transmitted even before the forming of broadcast radio. Transmissions of both live performances and records occurred, for instance, at an exhibition in Luleå 1921, as well as from small amateur radio associations and commercial companies during the first years of the 1920s.[9] However, after the wireless technique of transmitting sound was organised into a single company responsible for nationwide broadcasts, and with the introduction in agreement with the state in 1925 of general guidelines regulating content, the issue of music became problematic. The first agreement stated that *Radiotjänst* should produce:

> programmes of an alternating kind, provide good entertainment and aim at the continuation of a general interest in sound radio among the public. Furthermore, the programmes must be of a high cultural and artistic standard, be reliable, credible, accurate and unbiased. The sound radio shall provide services facilitating popular education. (*Hört och sett: Radio och television. 1925–1974*, my translation)

8. De Forrest, was the inventor of the triode (1906), which was essential for the development of the reception and amplification of a continuous electromagnetic (i.e. radio) signal.
9. During the First World War, music was also broadcast both to English and German soldiers on the west front (Schwitzke 1963).

These guidelines were obviously interpreted in favour of music, since the output consisted to a large extent of music (in 1925 as much as 51% were music programmes; Schyller 1996). The programmes were mainly live broadcasts from opera houses and concert halls, but sometimes merely relayed and redistributed broadcasts from other European radio companies. However, the programmes also included popular music, such as modern and old dance music, folk songs and ballads. From a technical point of view, though, the use of records was problematic: *Radiotjänst* did not have any electrically amplified gramophone at its disposal, and the arrangement with acoustically amplified sound and a microphone gave a poor acoustic quality. This problem was, however, resolved during the very first years when an electric gramophone was acquired. A more 'serious' problem remained, in that the preceding debate as to how Swedish radio should be organised concerned to a great degree the matter of commercialisation. This was because the political proponents of a solution strongly opposed any commercial involvement in radio programming and production, and thus, using commercial records as programme material could be regarded also as 'being commercial'. Furthermore, that music in the 'real and professional' radio was supposed to consist of live performances in the 'international movement of radio' (despite the commercial success of the gramophone in other fields) is indicated in a text written by Kurt Weill in 1926:

> The entire movement of radio is just beginning. Only long years of experience will reveal entertainment-radio's true mission. A special technique of singing and playing for radio purposes will develop, and sooner or later we will begin to find special instruments and new orchestral combinations suited to the acoustic requirements of the broadcast studio. And we can't yet foresee what new types of instruments and sound-producing devices may develop on this foundation. (Weill 1993(1926), 26f)

The kind of music anticipated by Weill was not the high-brow classical music of 'the elite', neither was it dance or folk music, but a wish that the 'radio concert' should form a new, more beautiful replacement for the earlier 'elite concert' – thus leaving little place for commercially recorded music (Weill 1993(1926), 28). Music was obviously of prime importance to the Swedish radio broadcasting company, because the music department was one of the first departments to be set up. Furthermore, the company hired its own orchestra from the outset, an orchestra that later became the Radio Orchestra and for decades a musical institution, consisting of sections such as a symphony orchestra, a radio choir, and a jazz orchestra (Björnberg 1998).[10]

It does not seem that any records were played during the very first year, and the first occurrence of announced music from records took place during a conflict between the musician's trade union and the radio company in 1926 (Björnberg 1998, 36). Nevertheless, records soon became a frequent part of programme production, first as 'space fillers' between transmissions from different live performances, but also as specific programme content. In 1929 a summary of the preceding five years of programme production states:

> Gramophone records constitute a novelty in radio programming. At the beginning records were used only occasionally, preferably in order to fill an unexpected and unwanted pause in the scheduled programming. Today they are the most popular type of programme provided by radio. (*Radiotjänst: En bok om programmen och lyssnarna*. 1929, 228, my translation)

The 'programme' referred to is probably an hour of gramophone music – which began in 1928 – played on demand from the radio retail business, which wanted to be able to demonstrate their radio sets. Since the company was obliged to maintain 'the continuation of a general interest of sound radio among the public' the hour of recorded music conformed to the agreement with the state.

Records rapidly became a considerable share of the musical output – in 1930 they amounted to 30% of the musical programming (CPR H1). That whole programmes were also based on records is obvious in programme titles such as *Famous coloratura-singers*, *World famous stars from cinema and stage*, or additions such as 'exotic music from records, including explanations' (Åberg 1999a, my translation). It is worth noting that the music genres selected sit, in a manner of speaking, on the fence between the 'serious' (coloratura-singers) and the 'popular'

10. Nothing unique to Sweden, as several radio broadcasting companies have a Radio orchestra, a choir, etc.

(stars from cinema and stage). These programmes almost certainly consisted of a programme host who entertained between carefully selected records – a form of performance without any obvious precursor outside radio.

Competing over the audience – music on request

Producing music programmes based on records began to change. Later on, in the 1940s, facing criticism of not providing popular music, *Radiotjänst* introduced a special kind of music request programme based on the live participation of listeners. This was accomplished by means of mobile transmitters: a car equipped with a loudspeaker and a microphone connected by a cable of considerable length to a low power transmitter in the car. On one occasion the programme host visited people on the third floor of a tenement house. In a way the company arranged wireless transmissions from 'events'. There were, however, other music request programmes on the air already, but these were mostly based on letters from listeners. As early as in 1925 an almost 'fatal mistake' was made in an attempt to introduce the use of the telephone for immediate contact with listeners, asking them to call the studio with their request. Since neither the telephone net nor the switchboard service at the telephone company were capable of handling this kind of activity, the attempt almost resulted in an abrupt end to the radio host's career as a radio professional (Jerring 1945, 32). In these programmes the requested music was played by an orchestra in the studio – records were used for inside production of a more 'sophisticated' kind. Still, the struggle to find a form that could reflect the taste of the listeners is obvious – the problem being to find a way of facilitating this very taste without turning to the commercial market. In this respect, the arranged 'events' of wirelessly transmitting live music complying with listeners' requests, was an acceptable solution.

These music request programmes apparently had something in common with the 'hit parade' programmes occurring at the same time in the U.S.; for instance, the idea of providing music of interest to a major audience, to some extent based on the music selected by the listeners themselves as indicated by sales figures. Basically this is one way of realising the competition for listeners, most evident in the development of formatted music radio in the U.S., but also appearing in the public service radio company's struggle to be 'popular'. David T. MacFarland traces the *Top 40* format to these 'hit parades' broadcast during the 1940s – orchestras playing the hits of the day, later on becoming both 'hit-list' programmes and radio stations' playing a very restricted selection of records, i.e. formatted music radio (MacFarland 1997).

Both in the U.S. and in Europe 'pirate' stations during the late 1950s and early 1960s did not provide 'hit parades' but 'hit-list' programmes or other forms of 'hosted music shows' providing music selected on commercial grounds (sales figures). However, these stations used exclusively recorded music, albeit not always records.[11] The 'hit-list' programmes of the radio pirates of the early 1960s also affected the programming of the Swedish public service radio company, which during this time had changed its name to *Sveriges Radio*. *Sveriges Radio* faced the challenge by launching three distinct 'hit-list' programmes. Also these programmes were based exclusively on playing records, but only one of them was based on sales ratings.[12]

The late 1950s and most of the 1960s was also the time when electronics entered the production of radio on a large scale. The technical equipment being developed at the time was based on transistor technology: professional tape recorders, cassette and cartridge players, high quality records and turntables, broadcasting consoles and sound manipulating facilities such as the vocoder. Most of all the tape recorder seems to have revolutionised radio production by allowing cutting and editing of the material. Pauses could be cut out and sounds lasting only for a second or two could be inserted or rearranged in a way never realised before. The final result became a

11. The 'most wanted' music was re-recorded on cartridges, the same type of tape recording that was used for station IDs and other jingles.
12. This somewhat 'commercial' programme was scheduled on a weekday, at a time held to be 'in the shadow of television' i.e. early evening time, while the other two – one promoting teenage pop music and the other a wide range of national Swedish popular music – were broadcast on weekends, at peak hour listening times, i.e. late morning and early afternoon.

smooth and seamless flow of sounds at a comparably high tempo. Apparently the competition of the edited speech also affected the live performed speech and cultivated real artists of a kind measuring up to professional auctioneers.

The combination of this novelty in radio programme production and the idea of 'giving the audience what it wants', i.e. their favourite music, later became in the U.S. the typical *Top 40*-format disc jockey show. A radio personality - a single performer with a special speech style - using the cartridge player for playing pre-recorded music as well as commercials, jingles and station IDs. The form of the hosted music show, intrinsic to radio's mediacy - solely *allowing* sound, no images, to be emitted - had now reached a new level of professionalism: the DJ show.[13] This form can be characterised in terms of presentation form: tempo, beat, striking jingles and sound effects; and 'radio personalities' or professionals with a specific kind of speech performance: people who could exploit the characteristics of microphones and who were speech equilibrists; their very performance being invisible but clearly audible to the listener.

The development of this 'genre' or programme type, probably originated with radio which, having its roots in events in society, such as public performances of popular music, transformed these events into music request programmes. While these public performances mainly provided music for dancing, it is certain that the orchestras occasionally played music on request. With radio the request programme was to become the main issue. Taking advantage of radio as a pure medium of sound, making this the most significant feature and combining it with the technical novelties of the time, the mere technology of distribution - the wireless - had become the delivery agent of a distinct form and content - radio.

13. This form and content cannot be accomplished by any other medium in a way as successful as radio. Attempts to transform the format to television - on MTV, for instance, deviates considerably after some time in favour of more 'traditional' televisional forms of expression - guests in a 'cosy corner' and interleaving short features. The very essence of DJ shows is intrinsic to the sound dimension of the form of expression.

Controversies on the essence of radio drama

Great expectations were held for the wireless during its first decade of existence; anticipations revolving around the emergence of a completely new form of artistic expression:

> In wireless the sounds and voices of reality claimed relations with the poetic word and the musical note; sounds born of earth and those born of the spirit found each other; and so music entered the material world, the world enveloped itself in music, and reality, newly created by thought in all its intensity, presented itself much more directly, objectively and concretely than on printed paper: what hitherto had only been thought or described now appeared materialised, as a corporeal actuality. (Arnheim 1936, 15)

That the dimension of sound and the lack of visual stimuli were prominent features of the wireless is reflected in one of the early dramatic programmes exclusively produced for radio – *A comedy of danger*. It begins with an electrical shortcut in a coal mine and then the story unfolds in total darkness. Especially in Germany a debate on the essence of radio, and especially the essence of radio drama, emerged which lasted for several decades (see for instance Brecht 1966, Benjamin 1993(1932), Jedele 1952, Schwitzke 1963, Knilli 1959, 1961, 1970). The main issue concerned whether radio drama could be held to be an art form in its own right, or if it was merely a derivative of literature. One proponent of radio drama, being a totally new form of art, even claimed radio to be a 'sanitary mission regarding contemporary literature', referring to the oral origin of literature (Schwitzke 1963, 33).[14] In Sweden the debate turned into more prosaic, but nevertheless artistic, concerns: the use of sound effects.

Interpreting the agreement with the state on matters of 'good entertainment' and keeping 'a high cultural and artistic standard', radio drama entered the programming sheets of *Radiotjänst* already in 1925, i.e., the first year of the company's existence. True to the idea of

14. 'Sanierungsingriff des Rundfunks in die Literatur', quoted from Schwitzke 1963:33, my translation. The statement was made by Alfred Döblin at a meeting concerning literature and radio in Kassel 1929.

radio being wireless transmission, the performances consisted of selected parts of staged theatre either broadcast directly from the theatre stage or performed in a studio (by the very same stage actors) specifically for the radio listeners. However, problems connected with fixed microphones and movement of the actors on stage turned interest towards exploring the specificities of radio as a device for dramatic expression – the last time that a pure distribution of a stage play occurred on Swedish radio was in 1932 (Nordmark 1994).[15] In 1929 a drama department was established and the managing director, Per Lindberg, was eager to turn the focus away from mere distribution; moreover, he made the development of radiophonic forms of expression his major goal (Franzén 1991).

From now on, radio drama, although often based on literature, would be modelled on staged performances only insofar as the coulisses constituted an essential part of the performance. Radio being 'blind' had, in one way or another, to compensate for the lack of visuality and apparently the most obvious way to do this was to transform the stage coulisses into 'sound coulisses'. Radio 'coulisses', i.e. sound effects, were produced live, often using equipment borrowed from the theatre – the most obvious one being the wind machine. In a chronicle in the magazine *Radiolyssnaren* [The radio listener] a foresighted columnist wrote already in 1927:

> The radio drama does not have to be satisfied with mere illusions. It can exploit the reality. By means of one or two microphones it is possible to get almost any kind of background or coulisse, from anywhere, and although not yet introduced – anyhow to the writer's knowledge – there will be no obstacle

15. The idea of radio being a means for distribution is reflected in statements made by the programme manager, who claimed that the staging of theatre especially for one single performance on radio would be a much too expensive undertaking, employing actors, etc (Hallingberg 1965). Moreover, the idea that radio was a mere channel of distribution is obvious in the organisation of several of the public service authorities in Scandinavian countries: a radio company for programme 'production', with the telegraph and postal authorities responsible for technical issues. Production was obviously understood as mere organisation and administration of the redistribution of occurring events.

in reproducing sounds recorded on gramophone records from which they, whenever needed, can be played – in the same way that a film reproduces moving images from a celluloid tape. Perhaps, in the future, there will be an industry specialised in this kind of production especially made for radio drama, or even for the production of radio drama as such. However, this is a vision of the future. (*Radiolyssnaren* 1927, my translation)

Sound effects were not only used in drama but also, on the strong recommendation of Lindberg, in radio features as well. A feature on some event in society could actually be 'scripted' in a way similar to a drama, with the participating interviewees making appropriate sounds according to a pre-written manuscript. However, the rather heavy use of sound effects was not appreciated by everybody! Listeners complained especially about the 'noises' making the speech hard to comprehend (Forsén 1966). Consequently, other ways of adapting drama to the wireless had to be found, the form of expression used on stage had to be transformed into that suitable for radio. Drawing on literature, i.e. drama in print, the solution became elaborations in the field of dialogue.

However, realising drama in the form of almost pure dialogue turned out to be problematic because this form was already in use in educational programmes and as adaptations of lectures to the sound medium of radio. The issue at stake in this case, is how to convey the fact that what is broadcast is *fiction*, not facts – the former practice of using sound effects also being a sign indicating the already known tradition of stage play and in that way also implying fiction. A problem perhaps most obviously exemplified by the reaction on the *Mercury Theatre on the Air* performance of H.G. Wells' *War of the Worlds* in October 1938. In a study of the event it is repeatedly stated by the respondents that the performance conformed so well to ordinary (factual) broadcasts that they took it to be real, not something imaginary taking place in a radio drama (Cantril 1940).[16]

16. The play starts with the last parts of a news/weather cast followed by a live broadcast from a ballroom. This music entertainment is then repeatedly interrupted by 'important messages' on strange phenomena occurring in Grower's Mill, New Jersey.

Scripted speech

Making the scripted speech the most significant feature of drama, one could argue that a monologue or dialogue in the form of reading aloud deviates apparently from a more spontaneous interaction or delivery, i.e. that they are different and distinct speech genres. Thus it might be held that a dramatic dialogue, as a scripted one, ought to be possible to distinguish from a more spontaneous one taking place in a programme of another kind. However, in Swedish radio (as in several other countries, I assume) monologues as well as dialogues and even discussions/debates were in a way 'scripted', i.e. speech in radio did not conform to ordinary colloquial speech genres. When producing a debate on, for instance current affairs matters, the different contributions were written down and actually performed in a live studio broadcast, something that suppresses the most obvious characteristics of 'spontaneous' speech and makes the delivery sound more 'written' conforming to 'literature read aloud'. Thus, the reading, i.e. performance, of a fictitious text had to be distinct, exaggerated in one way or another in order to be recognisable as fiction. The solution, fully established during the 1950s, became the use of a minimum of sound effects and modelling the prosodics on fictional film dialogue. A typical and quite distinguishable speech genre of radio drama can be found in performances from *Sveriges Radio* from the early 1950s and onwards. Its most apparent characteristics lie in the speech performance: few omissions, no false starts, notable long and syntactic pausing, a careful and clear articulation and an exaggerated and 'typical' intonation.

However, the development in electronics and technical equipment adapted to radio production also affected radio drama. In a way quite similar to the development of the hosted record show, during the late 1950s and the 1960s, radio drama professionals exploited the new technical devices along the lines of creating of something really radiophonic. Echoing the previous debate on the essence of radio drama, a debate on the reception and possible emancipating achievements of radiophonic forms of expression arose. The most radical claims, clearly stated by Friedrich Knilli, held the 'neues Hörspiel' to be able to evoke new dimensions of human perception (Knilli 1970, Cory 1974). The forms of this 'new sound play' were based on the dimension of sound, just as in the DJ show, and in some cases single words or phrases were repeated in a way resembling concrete poetry or Dadaism. Sounds were recorded and manipulated in a way that made their origin unrecognisable, or mixed sometimes in a way with the obvious purpose of juxtaposing phenomenon otherwise impossible to comprehend as co-existing (see for instance Schöning 1970, Kahn & Whitehead 1992). This development of radiophonic forms of artistic expression soon declined, but was merged with, and continued in the form known in Europe as 'electronic music' with composers such as Pierre Schaeffer and John Cage. In Sweden a special studio for electronic music was built and a number of recordings, echoing this radio development, were released by *Sveriges Radio* (for instance, *Text-Sound Compositions* 1–5).

Thus, in the development of radiophonic forms of radio drama a change of focus was necessary: from thinking in terms of a (wireless) distribution of staged drama (theatre) to adaptations based instead on printed drama (literature), giving the radio dramatic performance characteristics of its own. Starting out as speech surrounded by a large number of sound effects (coulisses) in the 1920s and early 1930s, it changed to being modelled on the written script of drama and finally on fictive film dialogue. Thus the Swedish radio drama got its characteristics – a very specialised form of spoken performance, with extremely well pronounced and articulated words and a very significant intonation. The same kind of speech can be heard in Swedish films made during the 1950s indicating a form of acting which once was perhaps a more common way of dramatic performance but which has become a sign of genre in radio, today abandoned in other forms of dramatic mediations.[17]

The idea of radio as a form of distribution is obvious in the attempts to exploit the dimension of sound in terms of sound effects, transforming an already existing form of expression (stage theatre) into another (sound radio). Discovering that the model of stage theatre was not suitable for wireless distribution the focus changed and literature and film became the main sources of inspiration. Even if radio drama is distinguishable from, for instance, news and features, the sound dimension of the performance still resembles other occur-

17. Radio drama is, according to several professional critics today, outdated and almost antiquated.

ring (mediated) speech genres. In taking this view it is possible to say that radio drama is a derivative of literature and not an art form in its own right. However, in the process of development of radio drama, it can be said to have given birth to another new form of expression – electronic music.

Exploiting the sound dimension

Interestingly, the fully fledged 'DJ shows' originating in U.S. commercial radio and European pirate radio, did not appear in the new third channel of *Sveriges Radio* in 1963, despite the channel being profiled towards a younger audience. One possible reason is the issue of 'commercialism'. The radio pirates and the debate surrounding the inception of regular television services in Sweden during the mid-fifties put once more the question of commercialism on the agenda. Because the DJ-show format was strongly connected to US commercial radio and European radio pirates, and subsequently to commercialism, it probably was an impossible choice of programme production. However, in the short-wave foreign service a programme apparently inspired by DJ shows occurred – *The Pops*. It was not the model of production that was 'copied' but the form. Based on popular music presented against a background of sound effects and other experimental sounds it had, nevertheless, the characteristics of DJ shows: a high tempo, jingles and an artistic speech performer comprising a never-ending and seamless wall of sound. This programme contained a carefully pre-recorded background, especially made for each programme, with close connections between the sounds in the background and the music or topics spoken about. Still it was a 'live show' with the (carefully prepared) presentations and playing of the records being performed live. Thus it can also be said to merge ideas of the time originating in the drama department with impulses from 'pirate' radio. *The Pops* had a number of successors and even entered into the national programme for a short while in the early 1970s, now called *The Kim and Roger radio program show*. The 'golden' era of artistic DJ shows took place mainly during the 1960s, however in Swedish national radio it did not occur until the late 1970s and early 1980s (with the exception of *The Kim and Roger radio program show*). Instead, during the 1960s the main novelties in programme form conformed to the ideas of 'neues Hörspiel' especially developing electronic music forms.

The major radiophonic era of Swedish radio was therefore the 1980s, but it was neither in the form of DJ shows nor electronic music. Instead the sound dimension of radio, its mediacy, was exploited in a number of programmes not only aimed at aesthetic pleasure or towards the younger audience. A number of entertainment programmes occurred, based on a lot of music, but where the music was neither 'requested' nor even the main focus. In programmes labelled *Good-night Robinson it is Friday*, *The Galaxy*, *Dream game*, *Water ripples*, and *Eldorado* visionary, fantastic as well as social and political issues were addressed in a form based on carefully prepared and performed speech, distinct voices, sound effects, and music chosen to be either a contrast, a comment, or a pure expression of mood. *Good-night Robinson it is Friday* had strong influence from radio drama since it was cast as a dialogue between Robinson Crusoe and Friday, furthermore it contained poetry not presented as a specific poem or of a specific poet, but integrated in the theme of the programme issue. *Dream game* exploited the ambiguity of sound effects occurring without 'textual anchorage' and can thus also be said to be reminiscent of ideas surrounding 'neues Hörspiel'. The production of the programmes demanded a lot of work, both journalistically and technically. As in *The Pops*, these programmes were in most cases performed live with a lot of pre-recorded items, not interleaving as in ordinary magazines but occurring simultaneously with the speech. Nevertheless, these productions also inspired magazine programmes, which, during the 1980s, often contained some specially pre-recorded backgrounds or inserts for particular issues of the programme.

Concluding remarks

These programme forms of the 1980s represent, from my point of view, radio as distinct from 'the wireless' because they exploit the mediacy of a medium of sound, wirelessly distributed or not. Regardless of the same content occurring in other mediated forms, they cannot be successfully transformed into, for instance, television, film or newspapers without losing their 'essence'. They constitute a form of expression exclusive to the medium we today call radio. Unfortunately, today, this form of production and thus the form of programmes hardly exists, and facing the Eureka-147 implementation with its text services and other kinds of visually focused characteristics, they probably do not fit into the current programming policy. However, in Sweden, one single exception can be found: the international commercial radio station *NRJ*, does not only play the 'most wanted' music, but produces its flow of music as a massive wall of sound. By means of about 20 station IDs, all of them performed by a female choir singing 'NRJ', but sung with a different beat, tempo and instrumental backing, differences between records are 'smoothed' making an impression of a constant sound. Rhythmic musical backgrounds are present during almost all kinds of speech, news as well as announcements. Even the succession of commercials and promotion jingles are arranged according to sound - the first commercial being rather complex, with several different sound effects, followed by a number of commercials with decreasing complexity. The commercial brake ends with news of some kind (new films, new albums etc.), and then the complexity is built up again (Åberg 1999b). However, this use of radio's mediacy is merely focused on music, not at all resembling the programmes produced by *Sveriges Radio* in the 1980s, which also included the expression of different kinds of content - often intentionally provocative and controversial - in their programmes.

My account of the development of these two radio genres suggests that radio's essential mediacy, without surprise, revolves around being a medium solely using sound for its expression. However, the preceding paragraphs also suggest that radio's mediacy can be exploited in different ways. Exploiting the mere sound dimension of radio in the context of art, and consequently demanding the whole concentration of a radio listener, seems to be a failure for radio as a mass medium, albeit not as an exclusive form of artistic expression. The great anticipations of Kurt Weill do not seem to have become real in radio, but in the development of electronic music of which radio has a prominent part. The novel experiments on 'neues Hörspiel' never became a success as a form of radio, but continued to exist as an art in close connection to radio.

Applying the idea of the sound dimension being primordial to radiophonic expression on popular and entertaining programmes, the forms originating mainly in DJ shows – and the DJ shows themselves, points to a form of radio both 'appealing to the masses' and taking advantage of radio's mediacy. However, the significant idea of radio in Sweden today being a 'sound wall' is realised mainly in conforming to U.S. inspired formatted music radio – without being an art of performance – merely making use of music as the focus of interest, limited to the supposedly 'most wanted' records. Nevertheless, perhaps the dialectics of 'old' public service traditions – with resources in terms of capability to allow time-demanding production, the training of staff, as well as pre-planning and pre-production – in competition with the commercial actors in the 'new' liberalised society, will result in new radiophonic forms yet to be discovered and exploited. One never knows!

References

Arnheim, Rudolf 1936. *Radio*. London: Faber & Faber.

Benjamin, Walter 1993(1932). Theater and Radio: Toward the Mutual Control of Their Work of Instruction. *Semiotext(e)* 6(1), 29-31. Originally published in *Blätter des Hessischen Landestheaters*.

Björnberg, Anders 1998. *Skval och harmoni: Musik i radio och TV 1925–1995*. Stockholm: Stiftelsen Etermedierna i Sverige.

Brecht, Berthold 1966. Radiotheorie 1927 bis 1932. B. Brecht, *Schriften zur Literatur und Kunst*, Band I 1920–1939. Frankfurt: Suhrkamp.

Briggs, Asa 1985. *The BBC: The first fifty years*. Oxford: Oxford University Press.

Cantril, Harold 1940. *The Invasion From Mars: A Study in the Psychology of Panic*. Princeton, NJ: Princeton University Press.

Cory, Mark E. 1974. *The emergence of an acoustical art form: An analysis of the German experimental* Hörspiel *of the 1960s*. Lincoln: University of Nebraska.

Elgemyr, Göran 1984. Radiotjänst och statsmakterna 1925–1957. Cederberg & Elgemyr (eds.), *Tala till och tala med: Perspektiv på den svenska radion och televisionen*. Stockholm: Legenda.

Elgemyr, Göran 1996. *Radion i strama tyglar: Om Radiotjänsts tillblivelse, teknik och ekonomi 1922–1957*. Stockholm: Stiftelsen Etermedierna i Sverige.

Falu rundradio fem år. Fifth anniversary booklet from Falu Broadcasting Association. 1929.

Flichy, Patrice 1995. *Dynamics of Modern Communication: The shaping and impact of new communication technologies*. London: Sage.

Forsén, Olof 1966. *Idyll och aktuellt: Olof Forsén berättar radiominnen*. Stockholm: Sveriges Radio.

Franzén, Nils-Olof 1991. *Radiominnen: Historia och hågkomster*. Stockholm: Natur och Kultur.

Hallingberg, Gunnar 1965. *Radioteater i 40 år: Den svenska repertoaren belyst*. Stockholm: Sveriges Radio.

Hinnen, Gerhard 1987. *Von Marconi bis Satellit*. Basel: Basilus Verlag.

Hört och sett. Radio och television: 1925–1974. Fiftieth anniversary book from Sveriges Radio. Stockholm 1974.

Jerring, Sven 1945. *På min våglängd*. Stockhom: Wahlström & Widstrand.

Kahn, Douglas & George Whitehead (eds.) 1992. *Wireless imagination: Sound, Radio and the avant-garde*. Cambridge, Mass.: MIT Press.

Knilli, Friedrich 1959. *Das Hörspiel in der Vorstellung der Hörer: Eine experimentalpsychologische Untersuchung*. Dissertation, Graz. Published in Knilli (1970).

Knilli, Friedrich 1961. *Das Hörspiel: Mittel und Möglichkeiten eines totalen Schallspiels*. Stuttgart: W. Kohlhammer Verlag.

Knilli, Friedrich 1970. *Deutsche Lautsprecher: Versuche zu einer Semiotik des Radios*. Stuttgart: Metzler.

Löfgren, Orvar 1990. Medierna i nationsbygget. U. Hannerz (ed.), *Medier och kulturer*. Stockholm: Carlssons.

MacFarland, David T. 1997. *Future Radio Programming Strategies: Cultivating Listenership in the Digital Age*. 2nd ed. Mahwah: Lawrence Erlbaum.

Matelski, M.J. 1993. Resilient Radio. *Media Studies Journal* 7(3).

Nordmark, Dag 1994. *Örats teater: Radiotjänsts teaterverksamhet fram till krigsåren*. Stockholm: Stiftelsen Etermedierna i Sverige. Unpublished.

Radiolyssnaren 1927, No. 7.

Radiotjänst. En bok om programmen och lyssnarna. Fifth anniversary book from *Radiotjänst*. Stockholm 1929.

Jedele, Helmut 1952. *Reproduktivität und Produktivität im Rundfunk*. Dissertation. Stuttgart. Unpublished.

Schwitzke, Heing 1963. *Das Hörspiel: Dramaturgie und Geschichte*. Köln: Knipenheuer & Witsch.

Schyller, Ingela 1996. *Radio- och tv-utbudet 1925–1994*. Arbetsrapport 1. Stockholm: Stiftelsen Etermedierna i Sverige.

Schöning, Klaus 1970. *Neues Hörspiel: Essays, Analysen, Gespräche*. Frankfurt: Suhrkamp.

Spinelli, Martin 1996. Radio Lessons for the Internet. *Postmodern Culture* 6(2). Also accessible at http://wings.buffalo.edu/epc/authors/spinelli/radio-lessons.html

Weill, Kurt 1993(1926). Radio and the Restructuring of Musical Life. *Semiotext(e)* 6(1), 26-28.

Williams, Raymond 1975/1990. *Television: Technology and Cultural Form*. 2nd ed. London: Routledge.

www.worlddab.org

Åberg, Carin 1999a. *Den omärkliga tekniken: Radio- och tv produktion 1925-1985*. Stockholm: Natur och Kultur.

Åberg, Carin 1999b. *The Sounds of Radio. On radio as an auditive means of communication*. Dissertation, Stockholm: Department of Journalism, Media and Communication, Stockholm University.

Åberg, Carin 1999c. *Is DAB really radio? On a new medium's status in relationship to established media practices*. Paper presented to the 14th Nordic Conference on Mass Communication Research. Kungälv 14–17 of August 1999. Unpublished.

Archive material from *Sveriges Radio*'s internal archive

CPR H1 Centrala programarkivet; Program- och sändningsstatistik 1925–1952.

Reflections on Writing Radio History

An Essay

Per Jauert

Introduction

The chapter on radio in the publication *Danish Media History* carries the headline 'Radio in television times' and deals with the period from the end of the 1950s to 1995. It starts this way:

> Danish Radio after 1960 seemed to be a medium in retreat, threatened by television and no longer the main inspiration source for public debate on cultural issues. But radio listening was in fact increasing and in the 1960s it reached a level comparable to television. [...] The real change was the new role of radio in everyday life. Radio took a background position while television became more visible in the foreground. Listening to radio became 'secondary' or 'distractive'. (Jensen 1997 (III), 178, my translation)

In one of the many reviews of the *Danish Media History* a colleague commented on this passage: 'How can we know for sure that this actually happened?'

This is the basic and simple question that one can put to any attempt to write media history – or history in general for that matter. And in this case a simple answer could be: I will know because I have access to sources which prove my statement: audience research, interviews with listeners, ethnographic reports etc. Or the answer might be: I have not had access to specific sources or material which can prove my statement in a strict 'social science' way, but by combining different kinds of cultural, social and political knowledge, empirical 'facts' and traces, this statement represents my interpretation of the history of this specific period in Danish radio history.

This way of asking the basic question and the two answers I can think of opens up for a series of theoretical and methodological questions. I will deal with some of these questions in this presentation. My background for doing so is my research related to writing the radio chapters in *Dansk Mediehistorie* (Danish Media History I-III, vol. 1-3, 1997).[1] Before actually writing the *Danish Media History* I-III the group of authors had to construct a strategy for the project. Our main concern was: 'do we know enough' to actually start the project and go through with it? What kind of a media history do we want to write and how should we deal with the many lacks or 'empty spaces' not yet properly dealt with in media research? Finally we concluded in a pragmatic way: we will write what we know of right now. Having made this decision we then had to find out: who should we write for?

It was our intention that our target group should be the interested and engaged public without any specific background. We especially aimed at undergraduate students in universities, colleges, etc. in the Danish educational system.

Before going deeper into the question of 'what kind of media history' *Danish Media History* represents, I will be more specific about the medium I was responsible for in the writer's group – radio.

What kind of a medium is radio, basically? How can, or must, these 'basic qualities' of the medium influence the decisions one has to make on the strategy of writing radio history?

As part of the strategic platform the writers decided not to deal with, or to trace, the history of the technology of each medium, but instead pay more attention to the technological interaction between different media and their social contexts in different periods of history, reflected nationally and internationally.[2]

Basic qualities of radio as a medium

When radio changed from a merely technical device to a social construction during the two first decades of this century many visions about the functions of radio occurred. These were partly put on the agenda because of the social necessity to place the medium in a clear

1. Cf. Jensen 1998.
2. Cf. Jensen 1998.

economical and institutional context. Should it be publicly or privately organised? Should it be a medium for communication (two way) rather than a medium for transmission - one way? The telephone was for quite a long period considered the medium for transmission while radio (the wireless) was considered too difficult to organise and construct properly for a listening audience.

The German philosopher and writer Bertolt Brecht was one of the first to insist on the communication qualities, not the transmission qualities of the new medium. In 1928 he wrote:

> Radio must be transformed from a medium of distribution to a medium of communication. Radio will develop into the most excellent medium of communication for public life you can imagine - a tremendous system of channels. This could be so, if radio were to be considered not only a medium for broadcasting, but also a medium to be received. It should not only make the listener listen, but also talk - not isolating him but placing him into a context. Radio has to give up its position as a distributor and instead organise the listener as a distributor. (Quoted from Thygesen 1974, 37, my translation)

These visions or 'the potentialities' of the functions of radio, were influenced by the way radio was organised in Germany and in most European countries from the beginning of the 1920s - more or less regulated by the state. Thinking of what happened in Germany just a few years later throws a certain light back on this vision. And the somehow utopian aspects of Brecht's vision are now - seventy years later - being revitalised in the recent practices of audio-casting on the World Wide Web.

Radio as anything else than an apparatus for propaganda was re-vitalised some forty years later by another German author, Hans-Magnus Enzensberger (see figure 1).

This functional typology aimed at a political change of the general media structure, based on alternative ideologies and implying collective processes of production and self-organisation (op.cit.) But indirectly it is also pointing at one of the core focus elements of recent academic studies of radio history: the reflection upon the specific qualities of the medium in its social and cultural specificity.

Enzensberger's model of the use of media	
Repressive use of media	*Emancipatory use of media*
Centrally controlled programme	Decentralised programme
One transmitter, many receivers	Each receiver a potential transmitter
Immobilisation of isolated individuals	Mobilisation of the masses
Passive consumer behaviour	Interaction of the involved, feedback
Depolitisation	A political learning process
Production of specialists	Collective production
Control by property owners or bureaucracy	Social control by self-organisation

Fig. 1 (From Jankowski, Prehn & Stappers 1992, 258)

Does radio punctuate and enliven the lives of listeners, as many of its practitioners would claim, or is it more appropriate to view the medium as an ever present cushion against silence or loneliness, as an aural tap to be turned on in search of temporary pleasures? Is radio a medium that is taken for granted – and is that its greatest strength, in that it fits in so well with our lives because it does not impose, impinge our demand too much? (Barnard 1989, vi-vii)

To connect from the structural aspects to the social reality of the radio as a basis for studies of the social and cultural uses of radio programmes is the main ambition of one of the most focused studies of the history of radio genres in American broadcasting, written by Michele Hilmes (Hilmes 1997). She argues against a narrow, structural and political science approach to writing radio history and instead she wants to base historical studies in a holistic framing:

This vision necessitates a whole new approach to radio's roots, one that attempts to locate them within the matrix of opinions, feelings, and interests within which radio developed as a technology, as a practice, and as a part of a lived daily experience, both for those who listened in and for those who experimented with its production: what Pierre Bourdieu might term the cultural 'field' of radio's origins. (Hilmes 1997, xiii)

These quotations - and I could have chosen many more - both encircle the social functions of radio as an organiser of everyday life and a companion in everyday life. Both angles stressing the fact that radio in a historical perspective has had a huge impact on the social construction of modern everyday life. Up to a certain point in history when the television set replaced radio in the living room were these functions changed and widened, but maybe not in a sense where you could claim them to be less valuable for the audiences?[3]

These cultural and socially based qualities of the medium itself - and the qualities in its social constructions - have of course an impact on the way you can trace it historically and write about it.

Therefore - let me now turn to the theoretical and methodological basis of the *Danish Media History* I-III and especially to the key aspects of the radio chapters.

Writing *Danish Media History* (I-III)

In general it was the scope and aim of *Danish Media History* to:

describe the contribution of the media to Danish culture [...]; their interaction with everyday conversation and the established forms of art will also be dealt with. [....] In media, popular culture meets high culture and foreign issues meet local issues. (Jensen 1997 (I), 9-10, my translation)

After describing the five waves of media history: oral culture, written culture, print culture, audio-visual culture and multimedia culture the main editor summarises:

3. The introduction of the FM band from the beginning of the 1960s and the invention of the transistor radio gave access to more radio listening for the individual outside the living room and shaped the background for the so-called new radio programme formats, aimed more specificly at new and more well-defined target groups - defined by taste in music style, genres or programme content (Jensen 1997 (III), 180).

> *Danish Media History* takes its point of departure in the new Danish and international forms of mass media research placing the audiences as the central link between media, culture and society of which they are part, and to which they contribute. The audiences are the bottleneck as well as the relay in media production and the distribution of meaning in society. (Jensen 1997 (I), 22, my translation)

In my interpretation *Danish Media History* is to be considered close to the key concept of Scannell and Cardiff in their unfinished social history of British Broadcasting (*A Social History of British Broadcasting*).[4]

Social history is defined as an intention:

> to describe the actual ways in which broadcasting developed and interacted with the society it was intended to serve; and second, to reflect on those accounts and their wider political, social and cultural implications. (Scannell & Cardiff 1991, x)

Scannell and Cardiff distinguish between different aspects of historical work. Historical work starts with narratives, but does not end there. The aim of their book was:

> to show – as fully as possible – how what we today recognise and take for granted as the utterly normal everyday output of broadcasting was, in the first place, actually discovered and set in place by broadcasters for listeners, in what ways, under what circumstances and for what reasons. (Scannell & Cardiff 1996, 1-2)

The general narrative structure of Scannell and Cardiffs *A Social History of British Broadcasting* starts with the formation of production practices and with the political formation of broadcasting – the institutionalisation of broadcasting. And it ends with an analyses of the broadcasters relationships to their audiences, how the programmes fitted into daily life, and its concerns for the listener.

4. Scannell and Cardiff 1991. A second volume has not occurred yet and unfortunately never will, according to the introduction in one af Paddy Scannell's later books *Radio, Television and Modern Life* (Scannell 1996).

In his recent publications Scannell's perspective has changed even more towards the perspective of everyday life. It is Scannell's key point:

> It [Radio, Television and Modern Life] presumes that making programmes is the *raison d'etre* of broadcasting systems and that analyses of programmes - showing how they work for audiences - are a central task in their study. (Scannell 1996, 2)

Here the lines of inspiration between the concepts of two recent national historical projects should be obvious. The concept for the writing of media history is for *Danish Media History* and for Scannell's project not defined within the structural formations of the media (technology, economy and politics/political economy), but rather in the media impact on culture and everyday life of the audiences, related to 'the structural narratives'.

From here I will now approach the more specific problems related to my own contributions on radio in *Danish Media History* I-III.

My intention for the first period (1920-1960) was to demonstrate the specific content and the interaction of those three central issues:

- The key qualities of the radio as a new and upcoming media ('nature')
- How those qualities were framed institutionally ('structure')
- How the audiences perceived and used radio: the impact of radio on everyday life ('culture')

In the following chapter I will give an example of how this concept has structured my presentation of the history of Danish Radio.

Danish Media History (II, 1920-1960)

Principles of presentation

What kind of story do I tell about the introduction of radio as a new medium in Denmark?

Beyond doubt, radio was the most important new mass medium between World War I and the late 1950s when television had its break in Denmark. Radio has probably been the medium with the most significant dissemination, including the later video and computer media.

The 'nature' of radio – in Danish settings – is strictly related to the potentials of the media, and can only in an analytical sense be separated from the structural and the cultural context. Radio was the first nation-wide medium to enter the private rooms of people, the first medium to transmit to everyone – simultaneously. In that way radio contributed in a unique way to the rising of a national media culture and a shared time and space: it provided listeners with a common cultural framing of themselves and their social lives. The Danish Broadcasting Company (1925: 'Statsradiofonien' and from 1959 'Danmarks Radio') connected the different communities of the country in spite of physical distances. The pause signal (the first part of a medieval Danish song, partly preserved in primitive notes), the direct transmission at 12 noon every day of the chiming bells at the Copenhagen Town Hall, and the daily news – the main newscast at 7 p.m. – connected the Danes in a shared time in spite of different personal routines. Besides being the vehicle of a new shaping of national identity it was also the first media technology capable of transmitting directly across local, regional and national boundaries.

The political framing of radio was influenced by the developments in the public sphere. In earlier decades around the turn of the 20th century the public debate in Danish media had concentrated on issues from the social sphere. Now in the 1920s and 1930s issues from the cultural sphere were put more in the foreground. How did this change influence the political discussions about defining the overall programme policy, the structural shaping of radio as a Danish broadcasting medium? These structural issues are traced in the first chapter of radio history in *Dansk Mediehistorie* (vol. 2) as well, and they are focused on the social and cultural consequences of the two main principles of organising radio, as discussed by the general public and Danish politicians at that time; either the BBC way of structuring the radio as a public utility, which later developed into the notion of public service (Syvertsen 1991); or the U.S.-mode, organising radio as a privately owned medium and as an integrated part of what later was labeled 'cultural industry'.

The cultural aspect of the introduction of the new medium was to trace how audiences perceived programme policy and output.

What did they get, how did they respond, and how did their conceptions of the programmes influence the programme policy during the period?

Sources on Radio History

Before going into more detail concerning my approach, I will outline the main available sources for historical research.

First of all it is not possible to find previous extensive research into radio. The most comprehensive study so far is a jubilee publication on the 50th anniversary of *Danmarks Radio* [Denmark's Radio] (Skovmand 1975). It consists of contributions from social scientists and historians and covers mainly structural, policy-oriented aspects of radio and television in Denmark from 1925-1975. Yearbooks from *Danmarks Radio*, mainly written by journalists, editors, directors etc. from an in-house perspective are a second important source of information. Often slightly biased, these yearbooks gave a wide range of perspectives on the cultural history of the shaping of programmes, programme policies and the growing paternalistic self-consciousness of the aims and scopes of public service: to enlighten and educate the population. *Danmarks Radio's* own archives are very incomplete and so far access to these has almost been impossible for external researchers. The archives consist of incomplete papers/documents, with minutes and reports of General Board (Radiorådet) meetings being an exception.[5]

Like most other countries the Danish radio programme archives are scattered and incomplete. A systematical collection of programmes was not established in Denmark until 1988 with the setting up of the State Media Collection, a part of the State Library. *Danmarks Radio's* own radio archives include 30,000 computer-registered recordings, including key words related to content, date of broadcasting, producer and other contributors. So far a systematic typologisation of programme genre studies - or for that matter any other kind of research - has not been conducted on the basis of this stored programme material.

5. This part of the archive has been the main source for Skovmand 1975.

Other valuable sources for *Danish Media History* I-III have been biographies written by 'radio personalities'[6] and some few contributions from academic research. Put candidly, radio history has not so far been a topic for academic mass communication research.

What Paddy Scannell and others have described as the main paradox of writing radio history is certainly true in Denmark: most of the object of research has simply vanished into thin air - due not only to a lack of archive facilities and archive consciousness, but also to the lack or non-existence of recording devices in the first decades of radio.

This limited access to sources and previous research has made it impossible so far to focus on the programme level in history writing. But due to the existence of *DR 50* yearbooks and written material from the wide range of Danish Audience Unions, it was possible at least to focus on the programme *policy* aspect of radio history.

'The Enlargement of the Living Room'

The following is an example from the first chapter on radio in *Dansk Mediehistorie,* and concerns the use of the three levels: nature, structure and culture in this chapter.

The title of the chapter is 'Hjemmets vægge udvides' - not easy to translate, but 'The Enlargement of the Living Room' must be as close as possible.

The chapter starts 'in medias res' with an analysis of an example of live radio transmission from a soccer match during the Olympic Games in London in 1948: Denmark vs. Italy.[7]

The focus of the analysis is the specific nature of radio language

6. For example, Aksel Dahlerup (1969) *Radio-Eventyr.* [Radio Tales]. Aksel Dahlerup was one of the most distinguished radio personalities in *Danmarks Radio* for more than fifty years - from the early days of radio broadcasting. He was especially recognised as one of the founding fathers of the special Danish radio feature, called 'audio pictures', 'starring' ordinary people in their everyday life situations.

7. The analyses are based on Kirsten Frandsen *Dansk Sportsjournalistik: Fra sport til publikum* (Frandsen 1997).

Fig. 2. Til Landskamp i Dagligstuen, *Blæksprutten* (1929), page 25 © Herluf Jensenius

and the main characteristics of radio as a medium for live transmission, and in relation to that, the impact of radio on the nation-building process clearly illustrated by the cartoon from *Blæksprutten* (1926) (see figure 2).

From this aspect of the 'nature of the medium' we proceed to the establishing of radio as a public radio – or a public service radio, close to the guidelines from the BBC and of course with Danish distinctive figures and sociological facts, related to the founding of *Danmarks Radio* (Statsradiofonien) as a cultural institution.

From this level of structure the presentation continues to the level of 'culture': how the audiences perceived and used radio; the impact of radio on everyday life.

In its first years the programmes were predominantly representations of highbrow culture: chamber music, classical music – and sometimes, though, more popular music, but popular in a bourgeois sense, i.e. transmissions from the bourgeois restaurants in Copenhagen, typically with a music repertoire of 'light classical music' from the Vienna period (see table 3).

Programme content, Danmarks Radio 1928-29[8]

	Programme type in %
Music	57
Culture	22
- lectures	11
- reports, transmissions	2
- drama	3
- recitation	6
News	8
Education	6
Children and Youth	3
Church Service	4
Total	100
Broadcasting hours	3.142
Broadcasting hours per day	9

Table 3

One of the early examples of audience research was conducted by *Danmarks Radio* in 1929. Quite remarkably it was not the numbers of hours or minutes that audiences spent listening to the radio which interested the Directors and the General Board, but rather the audiences' opinions of the programmes.

In fact, the public – when paying their radio licence fee, using a giro payment form – were requested to give their opinion of the programme genres. The result of this research was not published in extenso, but just a few details were given. The audience wanted:

– less opera transmissions, less classical music and less educational programmes (lectures, presentations).
– more brass band music, more old popular dance music, drama, variety, cabaret 'mixed entertainment': and one of the more picturesque demands was for 'mandolin, balalaika and other special instruments'.

8. Skovmand 1975, 331.

This audience research was named 'the balalaika study' and its results had a huge effect on the Directors and the General Board. Further audience research was not on the agenda for more than 25 years and was not taken up again on a regular basis until the late 1960s.

Until then, *Danmarks Radio* was in fact a genuine paternalistic, monopolistic institution, serving not the needs of the audience as expressed by the audience through audience research, but supplying what was considered to be the needs of the audience as defined from above.

This audience study and the long pause following it did not mean the end of the struggle on the cultural functions of radio. The following quotation from one of the leading personalities in the Social Democratic Party and later Chairman of the General Board of *Danmarks Radio* illustrates this. Peder Nørgaard wrote a few years after 'the balalaika study':

> The working class is not especially interested in opera and symphony orchestra music in the evening. No – after knocking-off time and during and after the evening meal it is a happy tune from a popular orchestra or a record that is needed. And after that – along with physical relaxation – it is a talk on political, social or vocational issues that will interest the working-class person. (Peder Nørgaard, 1934, from Ahm 1972, 13)

After this example of the class struggle of the cultural functions of radio, the chapter 'Hjemmets vægge udvides' concentrates on describing the programme output. This is based upon written sources, combined with the key developmental issues of the structural framing of radio as an institution, leading up to the changes around 1960 when television replaced radio as the dominant domestic medium, and radio changed its position from the centre of the living room to more of a companion in the kitchen, the car, and at picnics, etc.

Here the first chapter on radio history in *Danish Media History* ends, and a new one begins in vol. III covering the period 1960-95.

'How can we know?'

Now I return to my point of departure: the radical change of the social functions of radio, expressed in my statement about the change from intensive to extensive listening, and also the change of radio from primarily a main source of information, news and entertainment to a companion in everyday life with a more diversified set of social functions.

But the review I quoted at the beginning of my presentation, which posed the question: 'How can we know for sure?' had a point! I cannot be sure in a specific or accurate sense. But following the lines of the three levels of history writing that I have argued for and illustrated in this presentation: the 'nature,' the 'structure' and the 'culture' of radio as a medium, I am convinced of the validity of my presumptions – or, if you like: my humanistically based interpretations of the social history of radio in Denmark.

References

Ahm, Leif 1972. *En verden i lyd og billeder*. København: Lademann.

Barnard, Stephen 1989. *On the Radio: Music Radio in Britain*. Milton Keynes: Open University Press.

Dahlerup, Aksel 1969. *Radio-Eventyr*. København: Lohses Forlag.

Frandsen, Kirsten 1997. *Dansk Sportsjournalistik: Fra Sport til publikum* (Ph.D.-dissertation). Aarhus: Danmarks Journalisthøjskole.

Hilmes, Michele 1997. *Radio Voices: American Broadcasting, 1922-1952*. Minneapolis & London: University of Minnesota Press.

Jankowski, Nick, Ole Prehn & James Stappers 1992. *The People's Voice: Local Radio and Television in Europe*. London: John Libbey.

Jensen, Klaus Bruhn (ed.) 1997. *Dansk Mediehistorie*, I-III. København: Samleren.

Jensen, Klaus Bruhn 1998. Hvad man ikke ved: Dagsorden for forskning i (dansk) mediehistorie. *Nordicom Information* 20(1-2), 27-36.

Thygesen, Erik (ed.) 1974. *Folkets røst: Offentlig adgang til massemedierne*. København: Tiderne Skifter.

Scannell, Paddy & David Cardiff 1991. *A Social History of British Broadcasting*, vol. 1. 1922- 1939. Oxford: Basil Blackwell.

Scannell, Paddy 1996. *Radio, Television and Modern Life.* Oxford: Blackwell Publishers.

Skovmand, Roar 1975. *DR 50.* København: Danmarks Radio.

Syvertsen, Trine 1991. Hvem er mest 'public service'?. Ulla Carlsson (ed.), *Medier, människor, samhälle.* Gothenburg: Nordicom.

Proximity and Distance

Perspectives for Analysis of TV Fiction and its History

Gunhild Agger

A spectacular fish caught in Dragør

In October 1678 the Danish public wishing to be well informed could read about a spectacular kind of swordfish that had been caught in the sea near Dragør, and could even look at a drawing of it. The public could read about His Majesty's travels in September, caused by the ongoing war with Sweden; about the execution of a young virgin in Copenhagen and, in detail, of two murders in Funen, as well as recent events from the war. All in *Extraordinaires Maanedlige Relationer om det Nyt som er passered och fremkommen i September-Maaned.* The structure of the news seems rather unorganised to a spectator accustomed to modern principles of layout and content. Nevertheless, there are principles. One is the chronological order of events, small and great, indicated by the dates; another is the place from which the events are reported: First Denmark, specified in Copenhagen, Funen etc. - then other countries. Certainly, special attention is paid to the peculiar swordfish caught near Copenhagen.

The example demonstrates that proximity and distance have been essential as organising principles in the printed press from the beginning of its history. However, the ways in which these categories are handled vary from time to time. If we step a few years backwards in time, to the very first Danish newspapers, some of them were local versions of German newspapers, even printed in German. National news was not considered a 'must' from the beginning. The need for a national newspaper was gradually developed during the first years of absolutism and met by the poet Anders Bording 1666-77, again inspired by German - and French - examples.

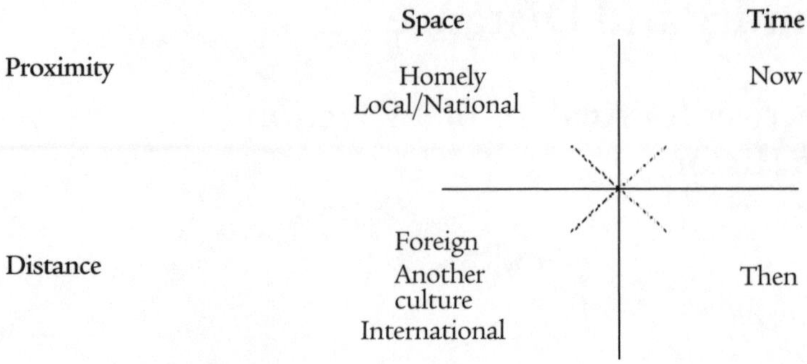

Fig. 1. Fundamental categories

The concepts of proximity and distance can be regarded as fundamental for media studies in several ways. As indicated, they already have a long history. During the nineteenth century the concepts became more obvious in structure and layout. They made themselves visible to the spectator in titles. An illustrated Danish magazine was called *Nær og Fjern* (1872-80, directly translated 'Near and Far Away'); the title indicates that the concepts were important for structuring both visual and verbal material in the illustrated magazine. Similar titles flourished in the popular illustrated magazines during the last part of the nineteenth century. In the printed press the model of organising news and feature articles according to home affairs or foreign affairs became more organised and self-evident. Obviously, it still serves as an organising principle there as well as on the radio and television. We have become so accustomed to this structure that we hardly notice it any more. Consequently, it might be appropriate to summarise its implications. Figure 1 illustrates the basic relationship between the categories which will serve as a guiding note in the following.

On the one hand proximity in space denotes the homely, the familiar on either a local or a national level; and proximity in time denotes closeness to the present moment. On the other, distance in space constitutes the otherness on various levels, the sense of foreignness, of another culture, international relations; and distance in space marks the past. But distance and proximity can easily be combined; this is marked by the dotted line. Proximity in space can be combined with distance in time, just as distance in space can be matched with proximity in time.

The example from 1678 concerns the organising of news, and it is easy to understand the impact of these concepts in relation to the long history of news or facts. Considering their constant and fundamental importance in this domain, it is tempting to ask: What about *fiction*? Can the concepts of proximity and distance be applied to fiction, and if this question is answered positively, in which ways? I shall deliver some arguments in favour of the idea that the concepts can shed light on the relationship between national and international TV fiction, the history and the genres of TV fiction, at least at a certain level of abstraction.

Purpose

The main endeavour in the following will be to discuss proximity and distance from three interrelated perspectives:

- the perspective of the imagined national community versus the international or global trend
- the perspective of the medium and its genres
- the perspective of concepts of periodisation and a concrete period in a Danish context: 1988-97.

In current theory television is perceived in two divergent ways: as a *national* medium, and as an *international or transnational* medium generated by and generating globalisation. If we go for *facts*, both ways are right. In certain countries television is primarily a vehicle for national productions, distributed by national channels (USA, India) and on a large scale exported abroad, especially American productions. In Europe, nations such as Great Britain, Germany, France, and to a certain degree, Italy and Spain, mainly broadcast their domestic productions on their public service channels, and to a certain extent, exports and imports take place. Especially Great Britain has a tradition of export that is promoted by the development of English as *lingua franca*. On commercial channels in these countries the amount of American television is more impressive.

In minor and small countries this pattern can also be found, but in a more blurred manner. Relative to size, cultural impact and traditions, production capacity and not least ways of financing, there are various traditions for national production in minor nations (in size of population e.g. Australia, Canada) and small nations (e.g. several European nations such as the Netherlands, the Scandinavian countries etc.). Domestic and foreign productions typically mingle on the national public service channels. Export of productions does take place, but on a limited scale. To complicate the picture, the audience in most countries have access to satellite channels of transnational or American character, and besides to a certain supply of other nations' channels, both public service and commercial channels. The degree to which audiences make use of these options varies and is especially dependant on age. These circumstances should be taken into consideration when discussing television and television fiction in a historical perspective: for small and minor nations a national focus must be supplemented by an international point of view.

If we go for *ideas* about national television and the impact of globalisation, it is interesting that we find divided attitudes. Examining the historical situation as well as the topical development it becomes clear that television has been considered both a vehicle for a common national culture and a vehicle for the opposite, for a transnational entertainment culture, at the same time. The reason for that could be that television under all circumstances is a primary medium for negotiation, which is the explanation I shall suggest.

The *medium* of television has a double character. It is a medium that has a potential for making a deep impression on the viewer, for setting the agenda and determining what should be discussed and what should not. And it is a medium in which the images and words are quickly forgotten because of its elusive and topical ways of working. All media, even the book, are dependent on a certain kind of topicality. But once broadcast, radio and television are more inaccessible and thus distant, at least when not videotaped.[1] Television can be said to feed on proximity, as it gets very close to people and can be very intimate; and distance, as everything quickly passes away. The concepts of proximity and distance are essential as categories for the under-

1. This might change with new technology, focussing on individual use of television.

standing of broadcasting because they catch the paradoxical duplicity and ambivalence of the medium.[2]

Television as an everyday medium delivers the proximity one can observe in certain everyday fiction *genres* (sitcoms, soaps, everyday drama). On the other hand, TV fiction always delivers a representation that is characterised by 'then and there'. This means that a certain distance is always inherent in TV fiction. However, it is almost not felt in the sitcom because of the audience who clearly have the function of diminishing the distance and of representing the real audience in the homes. It is very clearly felt in historical drama, which is remote in time though often close in space, the setting being, for example, London, Amsterdam, or Copenhagen. This distance, though, can also be considered a freedom: a freedom for the audience to mirror themselves in the past. As indicated formerly, proximity and distance are obvious categories when we try to map the structure of the news. Inspired by such attempts and especially by my colleague Jørgen Stigel, I shall map the relationship of TV fiction genres according to the understanding of the significance of proximity and distance outlined above.

Various concepts of *periodisation* have been discussed in connection with the development of television formats and genres as well as themes and aesthetics. The constant ongoing recirculation of old TV programmes adds a special dimension to the discussion making it increasingly difficult to find adequate criteria for periodisation. The connection between national and international levels of development does not make it easier. Nevertheless I shall argue that the period 1988-97 in a Danish context can be understood as a special period, characterised by certain traits. First and foremost it is a period of transition, from the dominance of monopoly public service television to a situation of competition between commercial television and public service television. And it is a period in which the question of national television puts itself opposed to, in competition with, learning from and negotiating with international, and especially American, television. This makes the period special with regard to TV fiction on a national level, and I shall delineate the contours of the most important developments.

2. Cf. Paddy Scannell 1996.

Television and the imagined national community

Concepts such as the history of national television raise the question of defining the relationship between nation and television. But there is no unanimous statement of what the relation of television is to the nation, or what television as a medium signified for national consciousness in the past and what it signifies today. A common point of departure for researchers in various fields has been Benedict Anderson's concept of the idea of nationhood as an 'imagined political community' (Anderson 1996, 6). In the process of developing the concept of nationhood historically, Anderson hints to the ways in which the system of electronic mass communication works. For instance he has an interesting note on radio: 'Invented only in 1895, radio made it possible to bypass print and summon into being an aural representation of the imagined community where the printed page scarcely penetrated.' (Anderson 1996, 54). Concentrating on developing the origins of nationhood historically, Anderson does not elaborate much on the role of modern electronic media, but he clearly ascribes a vital role in the imagining of nationhood to the book, written language and literature. Thus, a supplementary estimation of the significance of the electronic media is needed.

On a general level it can be found in *National Identity* where Anthony D. Smith lists 'a common, mass public culture' as one of the fundamental features of national identity, defining a nation as 'a named human population sharing an historic territory, common myths and historical memories, a mass, public culture, a common economy and common legal rights and duties for all members'. (Smith 1991, 14). A more detailed account of the significance of the media is not delivered in this context, though.[3]

We must turn to other sources in order to get a more precise idea about the relationship. In a Scandinavian context the etnographer Orvar Löfgren unfolds an interesting perspective in his article 'Medierne i nationsbygget' ('The media in the construction of the nation', with the significant undertitle 'How press, radio and TV made Sweden

3. In Agger 2001 I discuss the levels of negotiation between national, international and transnational levels.

Swedish', 1993, my translation). Taking up the cue from Benedict Anderson, he points to the radio as the most important medium for structuring the life of the Swedish nation during the period from the 1920s to the 1950s. This structuring concerns both daily rhythm and the festivals of the yearly cycle. According to Löfgren, television aspired to inherit this organising role, but it did not succeed in quite the same way due to a much more ambivalent attitude to it as both a 'promise' and a 'threat' (Löfgren 1993, 106). In a British context Michael Billig's line of understanding the national issue is close to Löfgren's in stressing the 'forgotten reminders' of national identity (Billig 1995, 8) and in drawing attention to the 'daily flagging' of the homeland in the political discourse of politicians in the press, on radio and television (Billig 1995, 96).

In a *historical* perspective it is pretty clear, then, that we find divided attitudes. On the one hand it is often regretted that television does not communicate with the impact it used to possess in the old days when everyone would discuss the same programmes with neighbours and colleges the day after they had been transmitted. This attitude would represent the 'promise' in Löfgren's terms. The feeling of sharing something, of *participating in an imagined national community*, is often represented with nostalgia. A typical expression of this attitude is to be found in the following recent statement by Mogens Lindhardt: 'Once upon a time there was a channel called "The Television". All of us watched it, and it formed a centre around which we gathered and discussed in private and publicly. Today television has receded to the private surroundings of our lives [...]. The centre is empty, and apparently it cannot be reconquered.' (Lindhardt 1997, 4. My translation from Danish). It should be noted that this description also seems to be valid for countries absolutely dominated by commercial television. Michael Curtin thus describes American television until the end of the 1970s as 'the primary mediator of national consciousness' (Curtin 1996, 182).

On the other hand, the same period is often referred to as both a period of *authority* or one-way communication and one of *entertainment* breaking through. The first phase of television in Denmark, from 1951 to 1964, has been labelled 'the paternalistic period' (Bondebjerg 1994, 45), and the so-called schoolmaster tradition that it nurtured has been the object of much ridicule, not least from younger and more informal channels. That the very same period was accused of being overloaded with entertainment, the 'threat' in Löfgren's terms, is intriguing. A radical expression of the critical attitude is found in the following statement from the Danish author Klaus Rifbjerg 1958: 'They [the producers] have continuously been looking at the barometer of popularity, they have glanced at the great American model and have adapted mainly bad offshoots: human interest programmes, no-good gramophone parades, huge throbbing, mechanical entertainment shows [...] never failing to dull the audience and develop a demand for more of the same kind.' (Rifbjerg 1958. My translation from Danish).

Perhaps, the overarching concept of participation in a mediated national community can be said to form a bridge between the opposites. The notion of authority is an expression of the civic and formative education going on in public service television, indicating salient issues and pointing out attitudes to them. The notion of entertainment is part of the same project of bringing people together in various conditions, conveying a sense of national communality, albeit often in an internationally inspired setting. Basically, entertainment deals with the concept of sharing, too, of enjoying oneself with others who share the same traditions and tastes.

In a *topical* perspective the evaluation is not unanimous, either. On the one hand, it is not considered so certain that the function of television as a central field for imagining nationhood has declined. The obvious and deliberate participation in the project of nation building that was carried out in radio and television by BBC and most other public service channels in Europe has surely shrunk. But there are other ways. What Dayan and Katz have labelled 'media events' (Dayan & Katz 1992, 5) can be understood as representations of rituals or ceremonies that are orientated towards imagining the national communality. Whether the occasion is competitive sports or AID-programmes, whether it is royal weddings or historical remembrances, television plays an active part in conveying this sense of communality. Louise Philips has recently demonstrated how the Danish media coverage of the wedding of Prince Joachim and Alexandra Manley on the 18 November 1995 was conducted in a way that supported the popularity of the monarchy without violating the egalitarian political culture (Philips 1999). Ratings from major sports events testify to the overwhelming significance attributed to the national issue by both television producers and audiences. And indeed, there is an abundance of other evidence pointing to the same result. The importance to a national audience of framing, of the well-known and homely channel voice guiding 'us' through the television evening, of national news and current affairs, and of nationally produced TV fiction seems to be universal (cf. Cunningham & Jacka 1996).

On the other hand, prevalent tendencies in present television cannot be ignored. They can be expressed succinctly by the keywords *transnationalisation* or *globalisation* (seeking a common ground for production and transmission of programmes), and, as a result of the first, *localisation* (seeking the nearness of the vicinity), *fragmentation* and *individualisation* (in programming as well as in reception situations). In countries formerly characterised by a monopoly situation, this is often seen as results of commercialisation and deregulation. David Morley and Kevin Robins describes this development as a crisis of identity, calling for new ways of 're-imagining communities' on a local level as well as on a national and transnational level (cf. Morley & Robins 1995).

It can be concluded that contradicting assessments concerning the significance of the relationship between nation and television are at stake, even if there sometimes are bridges between opposites as indicated above. The logical question, then, seems to be: How can these contrasts be explained? Both in a historical and in a topical perspective, television can be regarded as a primary medium of *negotiation*. It is a talkative medium; talk is conducted all the time in various forms, on the news, in documentaries, in dialogues in fiction, by the channel voice. One television genre is obviously based on talk - the talk show. And it is a visual medium; it has to show vivid images all the time. So talk and image basically negotiate: do they match, do they support each other or not, do they contrast? An audience is always 'imagined' by programmes and flow; it is often represented in the studio, again a way of drawing heavily on the concept of negotiation. Furthermore, the audience is addressed in many ways, directly and indirectly, by channel voices and studio hosts and hostesses. The audience is even referred to the use of other media, formerly the radio or the newspapers, now in an increasing degree the Internet for further information and chat.

Of course, negotiations are carried out in other media as well, but not with the same speed or sense of acuteness. In the national printed press, for instance, internationally inspired changes are often seen, but at a slower pace. Producers are the main initiators for bringing about changes. The audience is not as well orientated in the newspapers of foreign countries as in their own. Only a limited number of the intellectual audience will make comparisons on a daily basis, and therefore the demand for change seldom comes from the reading audience. The same is the case with the radio where daily listening to other nations' channels is very limited. The book and the cinema are media that invite international comparisons and consequently negotiations – especially the cinema because of its mixture of visual and auditive appeal – but they usually are conducted in a less acute way than on television. However, the audience is well orientated as regards television, especially in the minor and small nations where international TV is strongly represented, thus presenting a basis for comparison with – and challenge to – the national TV.

My assumption is that this basic capability of conducting negotiations at all times, at all levels, is one of the most salient features of television which can contribute to explaining the contradictions in the various assessments of television culture and the various functions performed by it. The various ways in which negotiations are carried out constitute one of the interesting aspects of the medium. Often this has been neglected in favour of focusing on the meanings, the messages and the reception.

In TV fiction these negotiations are carried out, too. TV fiction imagines and represents various scenarios as a whole. It delivers various options. It takes part in the debate without explicit statements of it. Choice of themes, genres, style, and on the whole aesthetics, are direct results of options taken and, accordingly, part of the negotiations going on.

Time, space and genres

The concepts of proximity and distance are at the heart of H. Prakke's News Model, which has inspired much thinking in the field of media theory. According to Prakke, proximity in time, space and culture are

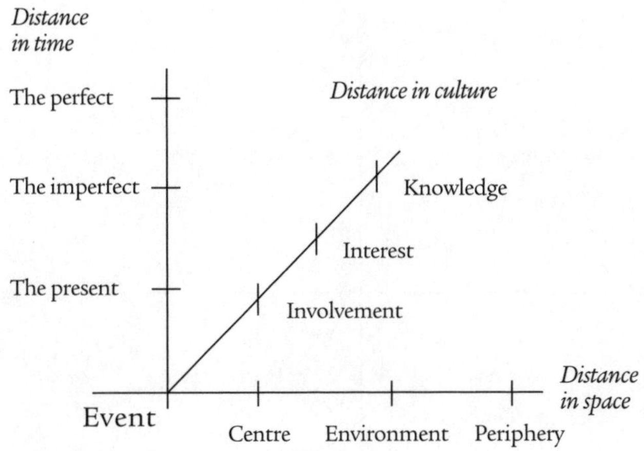

Fig. 2. Prakke's News model

decisive features from the perspective of the recipient when evaluating the news that is illustrated by figure 2.[4]

Following this lead Jørgen Stigel has elaborated a general model for television genres according to which they can be categorised in four main groups with regard to their relationship to time and space (see figure 3).[5]

According to this model we can distinguish the following main categories from their relations to time and space: 1) television news or on the spot reporting, characterised by proximity or even simultaneity in time and concretion in location (now/recently and here, meaning either locally, regionally or nationally, or there, meaning abroad), 2) TV documentary focusing on real events or problems at certain locations (then and there, but often with a salient topical perspective), 3) TV drama representing a past and a setting in artificial space (then and there), and 4) game or talk show dependant on real time in the studio

4. Cf. Prakke 1968, 122.
5. In Stigel 1997, 104. It should be noted that Stigel elaborates the model into a Cube Model of TV Programming, thus adapting Prakke's cultural dimension and elaborating it further. The Cube Model has its advantages as it is able to show complex relationships. However, for my purpose the simple model is more adequate in this context.

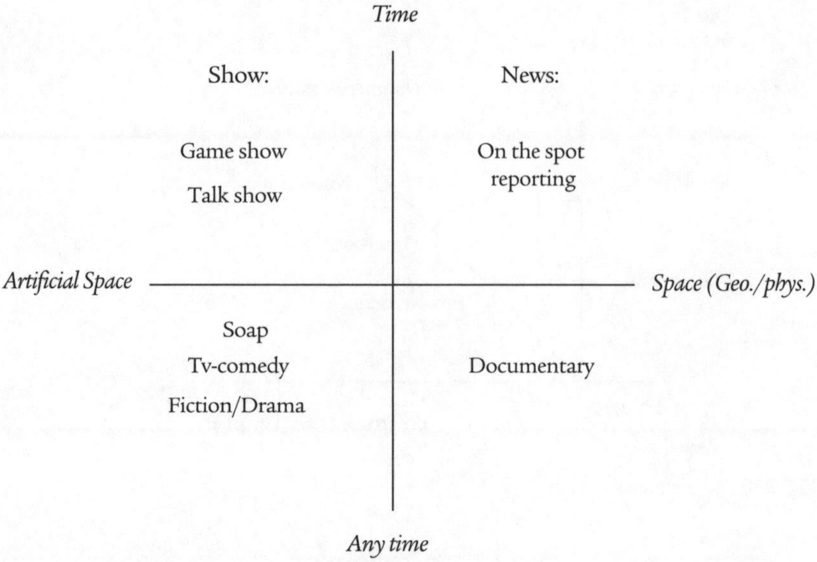

Fig. 3. Jørgen Stigel's Model of time and space in TV genres

(here and now or simulated as live on tape). No doubt this figure delivers a useful way of representing the relationship between various TV genres and main types. The key notions of my own approach, proximity and distance, are familiar to this way of thinking, and on the whole the approach to television, which springs from notions of the medium, invites to thinking in such categories.

As an everyday medium it is close to us. The screen, the channel voice, the modes of address, the language, and the flow is familiar to us, and so is the close up of facial expression or hands, conveying the feeling of *familiarity* and *intimacy*. On the other hand, as soon as they are broadcast the programmes *disappear*. They may be rerun, they may be videotaped, but the fundamental condition for the main bulk of programmes is that new ones in an incessant flow quickly replace them. They may have made an impact on us, they may still be present on the inner screen for some time or forever, but essentially the viewing experience is linked to the moment of broadcasting. Furthermore, we can interrupt communication by switching off, or we can zap between channels, we can make the programmes distant, or we can disappear ourselves, make us unavailable to all the addressers. In these ways distance is a part of the medium as well as proximity. A fundamental ambivalence can be observed. Whether taped or live, the programme is playing *simultaneously* with us, in our real time, and thus it is elusive (that is, when we do not video record it). On the other hand, it is a recognised fact that certain programmes serve as an electronical *memory*, all of a sudden making it possible to remember what childhood was like when recollecting a certain children's programme.

This goes for the way in which the medium functions in the private as well as the public sphere, and in addition for the way in which the medium undertakes a mingling of the spheres. It is close to the individual person, both when this individual is represented as a person on the screen and when addressed as an audience. Still it is a vehicle for groups and communities of various kinds, from the local or subcultural to the national or transnational community. These duplicities are fundamental for the ways in which TV interacts with our daily lives. It balances between impressions that become integrated parts of our electronical memory, and an elusiveness which calls for oblivion.

Michael Bakhtin in *Discourse in the Novel* (written in 1934-35), and in the essay *Forms of Time and of the Chronotope in the Novel* (written in 1937-38, both published in Bakhtin 1981), discussed from a theoretical perspective the combination of time and space in a genre context. In these essays Bakhtin outlines the principles of development as something which must be studied both in relation to a given period in a given society and to the development of a given genre, the vehicle here being the principle of dialogue. Later, in 1970, he stresses the function of the genre as a kind of memory (Bakhtin 1986). Genres have amassed a greater body of knowledge than the individual person, and new ways of evaluating the past are offered through the study of genre.[6]

Using the overarching concept of the *chronotope*, in the latter essay Bakhtin outlines a typology of the development of the novel from the Greek novel to Rabelais, giving a description of the various conceptions of time and space. The chronotope of *adventure* is thus characterised by technical and abstract relations between space and time, and by the reversibility of the chronological order and the mobility of

6. Cf. Agger 1999 where I discuss the teoretical issues and challenges inherent in applying the theoretical work of Michail Bakhtin in media theory.

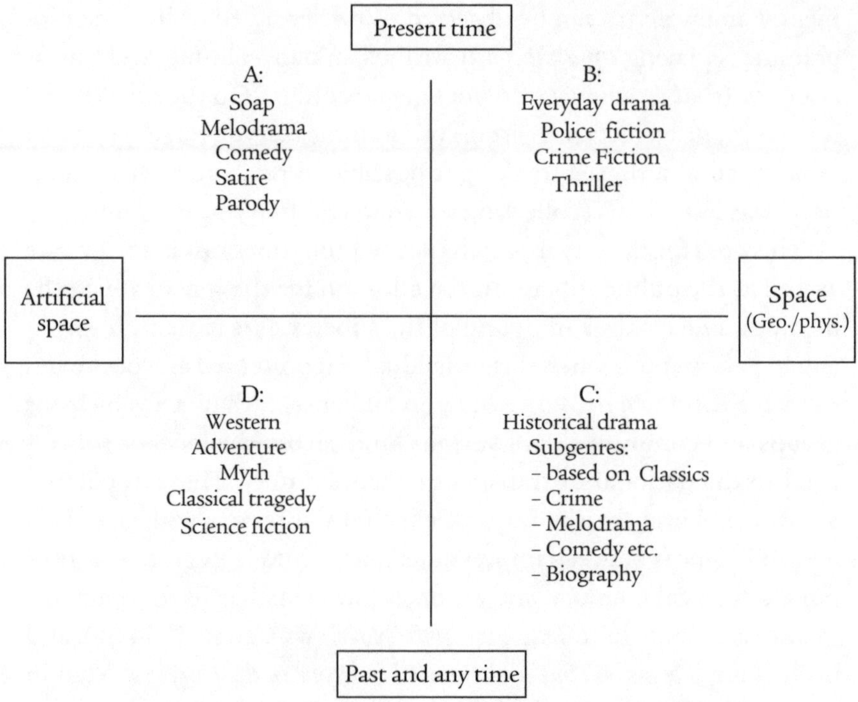

Fig. 4. Chronotope model of the relationship between TV genres in fiction

events in space. In the chronotope of *idyll* the relations of time and space change. Here, it is important that life has an organic basis in space, and the proximity between human life and nature is crucial. In this way Bakhtin points to the significance the chronotopes have for genres. He suggests that the chronotopes of the meeting, the road, the castle and the provincial town have an impact on the theme and the form of narration as well. Although this concept is linked to the development of the novel, the chronotope could prove itself valuable in the analysis of the special combination of time and space that characterises contemporary TV fiction.

The categories of time and space could be applied in a more detailed fashion in each of the four areas configured by Stigel above. For the field of TV fiction the basic pattern could be elaborated as illustrated in figure 4.

Each of the four new areas can be defined according to the combination of time and space, or, in the term of Bakhtin, the chronotope. Time in this connection is understood at an axis of contemporary time (Present time) versus historical and mythical time (Past and any time), and space is understood at an axis of fictive and in that way artificial space versus real and fictive space in recognisable surroundings where the real town- or landscapes play a vital role. In this way the relationship between prevalent genres of fiction can be illustrated. According to this a basic line of difference can be drawn between genres close to present day and historical or mythical genres representing the past (or the future as in science fiction). Another basic line of difference can be distinguished between genres which usually are played out in artificial space in the studio and genres which seek the proximity of geographically and socially recognisable settings and environments and use them as integral elements of the narrative.

According to this *soap* would be a genre characterised by a topical orientation, by proximity and the notion of parallel lives, where viewers have the feeling that they can almost interact with life as it is represented. The home and the family are indispensable conditions of the soap, mirroring the homes and families of the viewers. As a result it becomes increasingly difficult to distinguish between performers and roles, mediated fictions and realities as it is presented in e.g. magazines. The various genres based on *humour* are in a television context mostly topical and in this sense close to social or political contemporary life. The characters, the situations or the discourses are typically easily recognisable, but of cause represented with a twist, a duplicity, and thus a certain distance which is the condition of laughter. Often, comedy, satire and parody are performed as studio-productions before an audience. The combination between soap and melodrama is well described in media research; indeed one could claim that soap could not exist without the melodramatic excess. On the other hand, it is far removed from the comic genres in the same group.

This group of genres (A) share the topicality with the other main group (B). The difference is their orientation in space. Soap and the genres based on comic duplicity are typically set in artificial surroundings, in the studio or in a fictive setting which looks like a fictive setting also when it just represents ordinariness. The other group is typically set in a location which pretends to be close to real, though of cause in the interiors fictive, surroundings, recognisable in reality, the cities, the townscapes, the suburbs, the landscape (in USA for instance Los Angeles, Miami, New York, Las Vegas, the Mid West; in

Denmark: Copenhagen, Samsø). Though exceptions can be found, a recognisable setting seems to be the rule in everyday drama, police and crime fiction, and the thriller. The obvious reason for it is that these genres are preoccupied with social environment and the psychological effects of it, and on the whole are based on an expectation of a certain relationship between cause and effect. The thriller does not always comply to this; in this case it tends to acquire a mythical touch.

Historical drama constitutes the third group (C). A similar orientation towards real space is found in this group. A precondition for believing in historical drama is that the details are correct, that buttons in the historical costumes are as they were, that the streets are as we have seen them on old paintings etc. Although we do not know what the reality was like for sure, we are rather particular about the representation of it. That goes for historical events and for space as well. If it is supposed to represent London, it had better do it properly. Historical drama is the 'then and there' of fiction *par excellence*. Thus events and space become crucial in historical drama, for what else do we have? Frequently we find melodrama in combination with historical drama as well. The melodramatic mode seems well fitted to heighten the emotional appeal of history. Even police fiction can assume a melodramatic turn as it is seen in the latest developments.

The proposed distinctions can only serve as a guiding principle. All genres can mingle and wander between categories – and they do so incessantly. This is demonstrated most obviously in the case of historical drama where all genres can be worked out to function more or less successfully. Much historical drama is based on classic novels and provides a special duplicity, or often triplicity, of time layers: the time of historical events represented, the first representation in a novel, and the TV representation. On repeat showing a fourth layer is added. BBC has specialised in this during a long period with the Dickens' TV dramas from the 1970s; *Middlemarch, Pride and Prejudice* are examples from the 1990s. The percentage of historical fiction produced in Great Britain is larger than in the other big European countries.[7] Biography is another genre that has delivered material for historical drama. But

7. Cf. Buonanno 1997, 15.

historical fiction can also assume the shape of crime fiction (*Sherlock Holmes*), of soap (*Soap*), of melodrama (*War and Remembrance*), of adventure (*Dick Turpin*) etc.

Adventure may be considered quite an extension of historical drama, though, and I would suggest to place it in the fourth category (D) which also is orientated towards the past, but which represents it in another manner, loosened from the historical bonds. Adventure, westerns, myths, science fiction and classical tragedy share a preoccupation of a time that represents any time. The claim to be universal inherent in this is supported by the orientation towards space which directly underlines its symbolic values. Notions of the past and the future meet in science fiction.

During the 1990s, the question of 'pure' genres versus various genre mixtures has imposed itself incessantly. The example of melodrama is illuminating in this respect, but all genres are able to mix with one or more genres from the other groups. Frequently renewal is obtained in this way. 'Pure' genres only exist as models for producers, authors, audiences and critics. As genre research has shown, a basic distinction in genre studies is the one between 'abstract', 'theoretical' genres and 'empirical', 'historical' genres (Todorov 1978, 49). On a theoretical level, genres should be understood as processual, dynamic categories, per definition in opposition to any stability. But it is only possible to describe the theoretical level on the basis of the historical experience we have with genres and their development.

If everything can just change places, if all genres can mix, and if the relationship between genres is per definition instable, then perhaps it would be appropriate to ask: what is the point of a chronotope model of the relationship of TV fiction genres? Of course such a model cannot pretend to represent any final solution to the problem of fiction genres in television. At best, it might help us to figure out certain fundamental traits in the working of the genres, to make their interrelations clearer, and to explain the ways in which they match the medium and the ways in which they appeal to audiences. Furthermore, it could help to explain the relationship of the fiction genres to other TV genres. A consequence of the model is to point to, on one side, the relativity of Stigel's model, on the other side, the kinship between various forms of facts and fiction.

Concerning kinship, it should be noted that the game show and the talk show correspond to soap, melodrama and humour genres. Both are characterised by proximity in artificial space. News corresponds to everyday drama, crime- & police fictions and the thriller, due to their proximity and common orientation in a geographical and physical space. Documentary is characterised by being a 'there and then' genre, just as historical drama is; both depend on reference to geographical and physical space. Concerning the last quarter, the genres placed here are the most remote in time and space, and thus the ones which claim themselves most universal. In this way the model makes it easier to understand the character of flow in television, and also the ease with which we switch between genres, and between forms as 'faction' and 'infotainment'.

The relationship of genres, in fiction as well as in facts, is constantly negotiated, just as various kinds of imagined national and international communities and various genres in some degree reflecting these images. These negotiations can be said to constitute a *variable* in the model which operates at a level that is not sensible to anything but major changes. In this connection, the perspective of *other media* should also be considered, discussing the history of genres and the relationships between them. From this perspective, *constancy* is remarkable. Just as the news is still structured around principles of time and place, the fundamental fictional genres and the fundamental relationships between them are well known from literature. The classical main genres still figure in the model just as later developments from the nineteenth century such as melodrama, western, thriller, crime and police fiction. Later on all these genres are developed further in cinema. Only the soap can claim a special status as a genre that was first developed on the radio, and later in television.

To describe the special use of TV genres, it would be necessary to look at questions like the following: Quantitative information – how much is broadcast from each group and each genre? Another specific area of investigation would be style: In which ways do the various genres present themselves in television? The most evident difference, of course, is constituted by the various formats in television: the series and the serial being the most frequent, bringing TV fiction so close to everyday life, mirroring this life, and suggesting the notion of parallel lives to the audience. The difference between the media in this respect is not a difference in genres as much as it is a difference in the use of them, e.g. in style and in format. Presumably, these levels are crucial when difference between the uses of genres in the media is examined.

Seen from a *national versus international* point of view, the model can be used as an instrument for orientation. It is interesting to see if all the international genres figure in a national context, and if they do, what the relationship is between them - and if there are specially developed genres of national origin that do not figure in the model. It is also interesting to contemplate the historical development from this perspective. In a Danish context, for example, the incarnation of the television genre in fiction, the soap, has been developed only since the 1990s. All the genres in Group D are scarce if at all existing. The main bulk of TV fiction is contemporary, but focus has shifted from contemporary everyday drama to the internationally customary genres.

The period 1988-1997

As it has been stated, most television genres are international. Common formulas, common developments and concepts, common aesthetics are widespread as a consequence of the international market laws and the cultural transfers incessantly taking place. That is the reason why an international approach to the study of television is possible and rewarding, as in e.g. *Television: An International History*, edited by Anthony Smith 1995. Obviously, there are also limitations to the international point of view, developments that do not fit in the common scheme, genres that can be defined in various manners, etc. When the history of TV fiction is concerned, it is advisable to approach the development of genres on a national basis, but with a constant view to the international development. Concepts of periods and criteria for periodisation tend to be more precise on a national level, but one can never avoid the international framing because it is dependent on certain common patterns in the development of technology, in the institutions, in perhaps more vaguely, the feeling of contemporaneity. Although similarities and differences are clearer seen in the development on a national basis, the international framing is always useful for comparison.

In Denmark, we have various contributions to the history of television and television genres, amongst them TV fiction. Peder Grøngaard has written a book on *Det danske TV-spil* [The Danish TV-Play] 1988. In a comprehensive volume he accounts for the institutional history of the TV Drama-Department and he distinguishes three main phases in the development of drama, basically following the decades from the 1960s to the 1980s. As a chronicle of developments on an institutional level and as a characterising and evaluating chronicle on TV plays and serials it is invaluable. At the same time its scope and organisation could not be continued into the period after 1988 due to major changes.

Ib Bondebjerg has diligently contributed to the history of Danish TV fiction, in several essays, in *Dansk mediehistorie* [History of the Danish Media] 1996-97, and not least in *Elektroniske fiktioner* [Electronic Fictions] 1993. In this book the point of view is essentially international, demonstrating the common functions of TV fiction and its formats in various contexts. Especially the grand historical serial in Denmark, Britain, USA and Germany is the hero of the book, as it conveys both the feeling of time passing by and the remembrance. The international set-up proves itself valid and helps to explain the popularity of the great international serials, broadcast in Denmark as elsewhere.

In a national context Bondebjerg suggests three phases of development, and they count for the development of *programming* in television as a whole: 1) 'the Paternalistic Period' 1951-1964, when an educational ideology prevailed, 2) 'the Classic Public Service Period' or 'the Golden Age' of Danish television 1964-1980 when a broad range of programs and genres were developed, and 3) 'the Period of Mixed Culture' from 1980 until the period when the monopoly of DR was gradually broken (Bondebjerg & Bono 1994, 45-46). On the whole this periodisation seems correct in its main diagnosis of prevailing traits. The notion of a 'Golden Age' is inherent in other national television histories as well as it is in much media history.[8] But concept of a

8. Richard Paterson, in his contribution to the international history of television, makes use of the notion, for the early 1960s and the mid-1980s, simultaneously mentioning the possibility of 'misremembering' (Paterson 1995, 97). John Caughie applies the label of the 'Golden Age' to BBC television drama in the period between 1965 and 1975 (Caughie 2000, 57).

'Golden Age' inevitably implies the notion of decline, and I am not sure whether this is true of TV fiction (or for that matter of news or documentaries). Change is taking place, and it is important to characterise in which ways changes occur and due to which causes.

In Bondebjerg & Bono's anthology, Henrik Søndergaard suggests another division from an *institutional* point of view. He distinguishes three main phases: 1) 'the monopoly phase' from the mid-fifties to the beginning of the eighties, 2) 'the break-up phase' as a transition period during the eighties, and 3) 'the competitive phase' from 1988 when TV 2 started (Søndergaard 1994, 12). As years pass by it is not difficult to see that the phase of competition really meant a change, also for TV fiction, and therefore, trying to find criteria for periodisation in a contemporary context, 1988 would be the choice. This corresponds to the break of monopoly in other nations, dominated by public service television (Australia, Norway etc.); the time may vary, but the consequences are similar.

But when does a contemporary period end, and in which ways can we be sure to capture its distinguishing features when we have the proximity to the period, but not the distance necessary to make up a pattern? The problem with television is that its topical and elusive character has undermined preoccupation with its historical traditions. At the same time it is striking that the historical issue becomes recirculated with the old programs, to a certain extent confusing the boundaries between close and distant. This is especially true for TV fiction. In a contemporary context we cannot know for certain whether one period is closed and a new one has begun. In my context, that means that I cannot close a period in 1997. What I can do is to claim that certain determining traits, constituting the dominant key of the period, have been established, and that the TV fiction of the period, in genres, themes, and aesthetics, can be regarded as space for representation of this.

If I should succinctly point out which traits are salient in relation to the period 1988-1997, I would point to the following two:

1) The period gives rise to new debates about all levels of *belonging*. This is felt in the local-global perspective, and manifests itself with great impact on the level of the nation state. The impression of a breakdown of the wall and the following upheaval of nationalism,

on the one hand, and the experience with the European Union on the other, caused great turmoil in Denmark.

2) The period witnesses a re-grouping of Danish society criss-crossing the usual political levels that used to dominate political and social life. The welfare-state is being reorganised at all levels, a process which has not yet terminated; everything from bus companies to kindergartens and food for the elderly has become the sudden object of private enterprise, at least in debates, and also – sometimes – in reality. The ethics of both public and private enterprise is questioned. In the media an opposition between commercialism and public service intrigues the nation. On the whole, society is trying to find a new balance after the feminism and socialism of the 1970s and the conservatism and individualism of the 1980s.

These processes are thematised by the television fiction of the period, which in that way contributes to the discussion of what we are as a community and as a nation. This goes for various genres from historical drama (*Gøngehøvdingen*, *Call me Liva*, *The Brewer*) to everyday drama, satire and soap (*Karrusel*, *Flemming og Berit*, *TAXA*) as well as police fiction (*Island Cop*). The family Christmas calendars elucidate the national traditions connected with the apotheosis of Danishness, Christmas, and the Christmas calendars for grown-ups show the same traditions in a satirical light. Even *The Kingdom* can be regarded as a satire dealing with the fate of the nation and its crisis-hit inhabitants.

While the theme of belonging and various ways of imagining belonging is at stake, the formats, the genre models and the aesthetics change as a result of all the processes that are going on and as a result of international, American, transnational patterns. The 'TV-play' that was the rule in the 1960s, 1970s and 1980s becomes more scarce. However, it is still kept alive as a result of negotiations between cinema, the Ministry of Culture and DR/TV2 in 1994, resulting in the establishing of Novellefilmfonden, which is the main producer of the so-called 'short story' films. The diversity in the 1990s is represented by the bulk of 'novellefilm'. The internationally recognisable formats, most often rooted in American commercial television culture, has got a breakthrough in serials (which also were known back in the monopoly era) and series. As far as production is concerned, it is as a rule becoming international (Nordic or European), where formerly it was the exception. Imagining what it is to be Danish today is an endeavour undertaken by most serials and series, not necessarily as a main theme, but as an issue of significance.

The end?

Until now media history shows that the notions of proximity and distance have been essential for the structuring of the news, although scarcely noticed. However, these concepts seem to be useful not only for the news, but in other connections, too: As basic principles for understanding the function of television as a vehicle for a national or a global perspective, as an instrument of orientation for a model of fiction genres, and in connection with the developments of TV fiction in a recent period in a defined national context.

The opposition between proximity and distance lies beneath the current debate of television as a vehicle for national identity or global consciousness. I have pursued this debate on a historical and a topical level, implicating both facts and ideas. The opposition is of a kind that cannot be solved, but at least it can be clarified why it is so persistent. I consider the perspective of television as a constantly negotiating medium to be part of such clarification.

The character of television as a medium of both proximity and distance and as a negotiator between these levels can be observed in fiction genres at several levels. The relationship between fiction genres can be mapped with these concepts as guiding principles. The chronotope model of fiction genres creates a survey of typology and genre dominance at a synchronous level, and it is also useful as an instrument of registering developments at a historical level.

Negotiations with internationally developed genres in TV fiction have been the rule as long as television has existed, but after the break of monopoly such negotiations became salient, influencing genres and aesthetic thinking to a degree previously unknown. In Denmark this development took place during the period 1988-97. That is why this period is considered a good example of the negotiations between national and international levels, and why the consequences especially regarding genres and formats are so striking.

It is worth noticing that the fundamental implications of proximity and distance do not change overnight. On the contrary, the basic ways in which these concepts make sense, both as news and fiction genres are concerned, can be said to be unusually constant. This may change with the steady upcoming of various news services on the Internet and with new generations playing the same computer games, chatting and exchanging their own news in their own preferred fields, generations for whom proximity in similar subcultures across the globe weigh more heavily than local or national identity. Undoubtedly, the Internet can manifest itself as a stronger vehicle for globalisation than television.

References

Agger, Gunhild 1997. The 'Sideplays' Aesthetics. Martin Eide, Barbara Gentikow & Knut Helland (eds.), *Quality Television*. Bergen: Department of Media Studies.

Agger, Gunhild 1999. Intertextuality Revisited: Dialogues and Negotiations in Media Studies. Ib Bondebjerg (ed.), *Sekvens 1999.* København: Department of Film and Media Studies.

Agger, Gunhild & Alexander P. Nielsen 2000. The Good, the Bad and the Dull: Danish TV Fiction in 1998. Milly Buonanno (ed.), *Continuity and Change: Television Fiction in Europe. Eurofiction, Third Report.* Luton: John Libbey Media.

Agger, Gunhild 2001. National Cinema and TV Fiction in a Transnational Age. Gunhild Agger & Jens F. Jensen (eds.), *The Aesthetics of Television.* Aalborg: Aalborg Universitetsforlag.

Andersen, Michael Bruun 1996. TV og genre. *Kultur & Klasse* 80, 67-103.

Anderson, Benedict 1991. *Imagined Communities*. London & New York: Verso.

Bakhtin, Mikhael 1981. *The Dialogic Imagination*. Austin: University of Texas Press.

Bakhtin, Mikhael M. 1986. *Speech Genres and Other Late Essays*. Austin: University of Texas Press.

Billig, Michael 1995. *Banal Nationalism*. London: Sage.

Bondebjerg, Ib 1993. *Elektroniske fiktioner*. København: Borgen.

Bondebjerg, Ib 1994. Modern Danish Television – after the Monopoly Era. Ib Bondebjerg & Francesco Bono (eds.), *Nordic Television: History, Politics and Aesthetics. Sekvens* special edition. Copenhagen: Department of Film and Media Studies.

Buonanno, Milly (ed.) 1998. *Imaginary Dreamscapes: Television Fiction in Europe. First Report of the Eurofiction Project.* Luton: John Libbey Media.

Caughie, John 2000. *Television Drama: Realism, Modernism, and British Culture*. Oxford: Oxford University Press.

Cunningham, Stuart & Elizabeth Jacka 1996. *Australian Television and International Mediascapes*. Cambridge: Cambridge University Press.

Curtin, Michael 1996. On Edge. Richard Ohmann et al. (eds.), *Making and Selling Culture*, Hanover, NH: Wicobyan University Press.

Jensen, Klaus Bruhn (ed.) 1996-97. *Dansk mediehistorie*. København: Gyldendal.

Dayan, Daniel & Elihu Katz 1992. *Media Events: The Live Broadcasting of History*. Cambridge, Mass.: Harvard University Press.

Lindhardt, Mogens 1997. Om tv-mediets forenelighed med kulturdebat og oplysning. *Kritik* 130, 3-8.

Löfgren, Orvar 1993. Medierna i nationsbygget. Ulf Hannerz (ed.), *Medier och kulturer.* Lund: Carlssons.

Morley, David & Kevin Robins 1995. *Spaces of Identity*. London & New York: Routledge.

Paterson, Richard 1995. Drama and Entertainment. Anthony Smith (ed.), *Television: An International History*. Oxford: Oxford University Press.

Philips, Louise 1999. Media discourse and the Danish monarchy: reconciling egalitarianism and royalism. *Media, Culture & Society* 21(2), 221-45.

Prakke, Henk 1968. *Kommunikation der Gesellschaft.* Münster: Verlag Regensburg Münster.

Rifbjerg, Klaus 1958. Den nye pest. Verner Svendsen (ed.), *Midt i en Quiztid.* København: Gyldendal.

Scannell, Paddy 1996. *Radio, Television and Modern Life*. Oxford: Blackwell.

Scannell, Paddy & David Cardiff 1997. The National Culture. Oliver Boyd-Barrett & Chris Newbold (eds.), *Approaches to Media.* London: Arnold.

Smith, Anthony D. 1991. *National Identity*. London: Penquin Books.

Stigel, Jørgen 1997. The Aesthetics of Television, the Quality of Television: On distinctions and Relations of Programme Form and Quality of Address. Martin Eide, Barbara Gentikow & Knut Helland (eds.), *Quality Television.* Bergen: Department of Media Studies.

Søndergaard, Henrik 1994. Fundamentals in the History of Danish Television. Ib Bondebjerg & Francesco Bono (eds.), *Nordic Television: History, Politics and Aesthetics, Sekvens* special edition. Copenhagen: Department of Film and Media Studies.

Todorov, Tzvetan 1978. L'origine des genres. Tzvetan Todorov, *Les genres du discours.* Paris: Éditions du Seuil.

National Identity and the Dutch Monarchy in Historical Fiction

Revisioning 'The Family on the Throne'

Sonja de Leeuw

Introduction

Since the end of the 1980s and in the 1990s identity has appeared in the heart of the debate on social theory and cultural studies. It represents a strong need to discuss personal and political questions of identity within the cultural debate. Drawing upon Gramsci, Rutherford argues that 'identity marks the conjuncture of our past with the social, cultural and economic relations we live within' (Rutherford 1990, 19). And as Jeffrey Weeks (1990) observes, identities are not neutral, but contain different and often conflicting values 'which touch upon fundamental, and deeply felt, issues about who we are and what we want to be and become. They also pose major political questions: how to achieve reconciliation between our collective needs as human beings and our specific needs as individuals and members of diverse communities, how to balance the universal and the particular' (Weeks 1990, 89). What is important here is that identity deals with the relationship between individuals and the social world. Identity then is socially constructed, its character dynamic and therefore changeable (Hall 1990 and 1993).

The debates that arose on national identity are indebted to the discourse of postmodernism, focussing on aspects of globalisation and fragmentation, which were supposed to threaten the concept of the nation state. The construction of national identity, from this point of view refers to processes of homogenisation and unification, regarded to be necessary in building the nation out of heterogeneous communities. Anderson (Anderson 1983) has convincingly argued that nations are *imagined communities* and that institutions like the media help people to participate in and integrate into these communities. The more general point I want to address in this article concerns the role of media, especially television, in the construction of national identity.

Television plays a powerful role in the construction of identity. It provides different groups with different identities (local, ethnic, regional specific) by pointing at relevant differences. On the other hand, television is capable of homogenising differences, mobilising collective experiences into less specific social identities that appeal to a whole nation. To study how 'national issues' like the monarchy are represented on television might be helpful for an understanding of processes of identity construction at specific historical moments. My focus here is on the production-text relationship. Given, the specific organisation of the Dutch broadcasting system, to which I will revert later, I am mainly interested in how broadcasting companies, scriptwriters and directors have used spaces for specific cultural production and in the dynamics that can be observed between, for example, broadcasters and filmmakers in realising their specific cultural mission. More specifically this article discusses how a particular cultural text, historical television drama on the monarchy, relates to notions of national identity. Thus, the focus will be on the history of representations of the monarchy in television drama. I suggest that dramatised versions of Dutch monarchy in the Netherlands do not follow a clear 'royalist discourse' (Phillips 1999) in the sense of an unquestioning loyalty to the monarchy, but rather present a revisioning of the royal family as a symbol of the nation.

Representation and historical fiction

Representation is one of the crucial aspects of the relationship between media and society: in what way, by whom and in which context are certain meanings provided by and given to images?

Speaking about representation, fiction, historical fiction, comes to the fore. One of the vital elements in a national public service television culture is providing people with fictional stories about their reality, about their history and the history of everyone who came to live next door. As David Morley puts it: 'it is a question of recognising the role of the stories we tell ourselves about our past in constructing our identities in the present' (Morley 1995, 91). As a bridge between present and past, historical fiction is capable of representing a diverse collection of stories about Dutch history and at the same time of intensifying the idea of the nation. In my current research I have studied two cases that by definition have a strong national appeal: World War II (De Leeuw 1999) and the monarchy, the latter of which I present here. How is the monarchy in historical fiction used to underscore and express the idea of national identity, if at all? Are notions of a common history created and are these projected on to the Dutch monarchy?

Historical reality only exists in its representation. Representing history, means by definition engaging in the ongoing discourse of history. Evidently, historical fiction recounts the past with its own rules (Rosenstone 1995): from traditional realist narrative conventions to modernist and post-modernist representational modes, characterised by fragmentation, the exploding of the conventions of the traditional tale and the splitting of narrative functions (White 1996; Burgoyne 1996). Staiger (Staiger 1996) takes us one step ahead in her plea for postmodern fiction as a method for representing history: she quotes Linda Hutcheon by suggesting that postmodern fiction does not disconnect itself from history, but asks the readers to question the process by which we represent ourselves and the world and to become aware of the means by which we make sense of experiences in our culture.

In representing the past the writer, director and producer take up historiographical responsibility. Virtually the crux of the whole question is how broadcasters and film and television makers interfere in the existing representational traditions of history, in this case, of the monarchy.

Monarchy, power, representation

I will now turn to the monarchy. In order to answer some of the questions mentioned earlier, I need to provide the most relevant aspects of the cultural and historical context of this topic and make a little excursion into Dutch history.

One of the characteristics of the Netherlands is its low nationalistic profile. This small country by the sea, main port to the world, has always been – and still is – a transito society with a transito culture, in which openness, an international orientation and a pragmatic attitude are prominent. I don't want, however, to fall into cultural generalisations that could easily be derived from the economic position of the Netherlands as a main port; indeed cultural media historians should even try to avoid such generalisations. On the other hand, labels like consensus society, where merchant and vicar are walking hand-in-hand, are used to keep up a specific 'national' profile against the outside world. In the first place, the notion of the Dutch being 'water managers' plays an important role in this profile. Strikingly enough, the Dutch crown prince Willem Alexander has chosen exactly water management as his present and future field of interest.

As a consequence of its transito culture, the Netherlands had and still has a long history of migration, reflected in its very pluriform society, accommodating a diversity of people, colours, religions and belief systems. It is considered to be our most precious cultural property. In other words: tolerance, non-discrimination and respect for cultural diversity (Van Thijn 1997). It is not that easy, though, to keep up these virtues in daily life. As Van Thijn puts it, in a world of difference, it is precisely difference that is a source of instability. The development of common, non-moralistic values and norms is but one way to cope with it.

Every country needs a national day to emphasise unity, the feeling of togetherness. Queen's Day in the Netherlands is such a day and probably because of the low nationalistic Dutch profile it is celebrated very enthusiastically, if not from the very beginning of its tradition. Queen's Day probably represents these common values and norms, if only for one day.

April 30th is Queen's Day in the Netherlands. It is the birthday of the present Queen's mother, Juliana. It remained Queen's Day after her abdication in 1980. On Queen's Day, the Netherlands turns orange (our royal family belongs to the House of Orange), and everyone has a day off. People are allowed to sell all kinds of things on the so-called free market: you just take your place along the street, put down your stuff and try to sell it before the sun goes down, after which you take what is not sold home again. Typically, low prices are the 'order of the day': happy people who respect each other, sharing the feeling of belonging to one nation.

Queen's Day has become a tradition, which was invented about a hundred years ago to present the monarchy in a specific way. As an *invented tradition* Queen's Day refers to a common constructed past. It can be explained by looking at the political situation at the end of the 19th century. Briefly summarised: the extension of the franchise gave the masses the possibility of voting, which was looked upon by liberal politicians as a potential polarisation within the national union, and this could be a threat to the homogeneous liberal culture. That is one of the reasons why they looked for symbols that could appeal to all groups in society. One of these symbols was the monarchy (De Jong 1998, 72).

Wilhelmina's birthday was a nice opportunity of creating a national Orange public holiday. Moreover it fit in with the efforts of Queen Emma, Wilhelmina's mother, to upgrade royalty. She had a strong feeling for new rituals and new traditions, and Queen's Day was one of these. Since her arrival in the Netherlands and the birth of her daughter Wilhelmina in 1880, funerals, inaugurations, marriages and the like were carried out and represented in a royal way! Especially the inauguration of Queen Wilhelmina (Emma's daughter) in 1898, and the birth of Princess Juliana (Wilhelmina's daughter) in 1909, received enthusiastic attention: throughout the country people could join orange parties. In fact they celebrated the continuation of the Orange dynasty. Emma and her advisors carefully constructed the image of a nice, civilised royal family, devoted to the Netherlands, and in order to disseminate this image they used the new mass media (first press, later radio and then television). It was important that this image could be enjoyed by, and spread to, as many people as possible. Later, Emma's daughter (Wilhelmina), granddaughter (Juliana) and great granddaughter (our present Queen Beatrix) all choose their own position on the delicate balance between 'ordinary' and 'special', between 'near the people' and 'keeping distance', a balance in tune with television; a balance capable of supporting the symbolic function of the monarchy.

Especially since Juliana, whose reigning period (1948-1980) runs parallel to the flourishing of the audio-visual era, the monarchy became more human: Juliana more or less symbolised 'the mother of Holland' character and on her Queen's Days people came to the royal palace to bring flowers and march along the royal steps, while in the garden all sorts of activities took place. Her daughter Beatrix, our present queen, changed the image of the 'mother' into that of the 'manager' reigning much more at a distance. On Queen's Day, however, she goes with her family to the people, every year in a different part of the Netherlands; she visits activities, moves among the people, and meets all sorts of groups that represent the cultural diversity of the Netherlands.

Queen's Day became a national event, maybe even a national ritual, from the first time it was broadcast live on television. National rituals in the Netherlands, the World War II memorial service on the 4th of May, for example, create an experience of social cohesion. These national rituals can become what Dayan and Katz call 'coronations', ceremonial broadcasts, like the coronation of a monarch. However, these 'coronations' characterise inaugurations of all sorts, such as official funerals and commemorations. As integrative forms of information and entertainment, such coronations 'illustrate the working of collective norms [...]; they signify a commitment to existing norms' (Dayan & Katz 1995, 179). Their function is to call to mind the continuity of a society focussing on national identity. On Queen's Day the monarchy represents precisely this function, expressed through the notion of 'the family on the throne'. As Phillips (Phillips 1999, 226) has pointed out, in the case of Denmark, the idea of the family on the throne, representing the Danish people as family, was reinforced by publicly presenting the royal family as ordinary. She links this kind of representation with the democratic and egalitarian nature of Danish society, apart from the role of media in constructing this positive image of royalty.

This also applies to the Dutch situation, and precisely the live television broadcast of Queen's Day invokes the idea of 'nation' through its obvious loyalty to the royal family and the monarchy itself. In the terms of Dayan and Katz, Queen's Day can be identified as a coronation. By publicly presenting a living and vital royal family who are 'with us', the continuity of the monarchy is celebrated and through it the continuity of Dutch society. Moreover on Queen's Day culturally diverse communities in the Netherlands are invited to openly demonstrate their commitment to Dutch collective norms (like tolerance, Van Thijn 1997), represented by the royal family.

The notion of 'the family on the throne', with whom it is easier for people to identify than with ever-changing politicians, was strengthened during the last 150 years as a counterbalance to the loss of political power (Diependaal 1998). Since there is no direct contact between people and king or queen, the representation of royalty is of great importance for the confirmation of monarchic power. During the last 150 years monarchic power declined because of processes of democratisation. In this context Diependaal (ibid., 69) refers to Walter Bagehot, who wrote his famous *The English Constitution* in 1867. Bagehot noted that the political function of the crown was reduced to three rights: the right to be consulted, the right to encourage, the right to warn.

These words also apply to the Dutch situation, but in the Netherlands, the Queen has the right to make the political formation of the government (because of our system of political coalition government). Besides she has a weekly meeting with the Prime Minister and regular meetings with the members of the Second Chamber (comparable to the House of Commons in the UK), and as in the UK, the Queen reads the 'Queen's Speech' at the beginning of the parliamentary year. Although the Queen's function is limited politically, it is not only a decorative one.

The notion of 'the family on the throne' was carried out by emphasising not so much the political and human characteristics of the monarch, but because the private life of the monarch became partly 'public', a position that carries a constant risk of unwelcome representations (as we have seen for example in the UK). To minimise this risk, media representations of the royal family in the Netherlands are controlled by the Government Information Service, the official institute exclusively entrusted with the protection of the royal family. But this service has no control over autonomous representations like historical fiction, apart from the fact that it can, and does, prohibit the filming of the royal offices, even the exteriors and the consulting of certain royal archives, necessary for research. And it has to be said that among other things this reluctant attitude has limited the quantity and scope of historical fiction on the monarchy.

Different approaches

If we now take a closer look at the production practice of historical fiction and the monarchy, a few general observations can be made. All productions were broadcast on public service channels. In public service channels, programmes are made to serve the audience; viewers are addressed as citizens not as consumers. Because of this specific position, public broadcasting has a cultural mission like, for example, stimulating 'national' culture in all its diversity, reflecting the pluriformity of Dutch society and its changes.

Pluriformity as a defining concept of Dutch society is reflected in the Dutch broadcasting system; its unique character is under change as a result of commercial broadcasting. However the concept of pluriformity still is – and will be – the main principle for organising public broadcasting programming, and in this respect it is very much different from other European public services such as those in Great Britain, Scandinavia or Germany. The history of public broadcasting in the Netherlands goes back to the 1920s when important religious and social currents in the Netherlands (neutral, Catholic, socialist, Protestant) took the initiative of founding broadcasting organisations with membership (through subscribers). Dutch society in those days was marked by the concept of pillarisation, a way of realising pluriformity. Although all of these early-founded companies still exist, they are no longer exclusively bound up with specific pillars in society. Besides, nowadays people tend more and more to organise themselves into different social and cultural (less religious) groups, which can no longer be defined in a very specific way. Cross-cultural interests reflect the Dutch social-cultural landscape as a whole, including its traditions as well as its new tendencies! At this moment eight Dutch public service broadcasting companies operate on three public channels, and by law they are obligated to provide a full range of programmes (containing cultural, educational, informative and entertainment parts in reasonable proportions). Moreover they are still obliged to represent certain religious, cultural, spiritual and social currents in their programmes. Here the legacy of pillarisation is still visible, albeit somewhat blurred. Broadcasting companies adapted their beliefs according to the social and cultural changes that took place in the course of years.

As to production practice itself, different approaches can be discerned:

1) In several productions the monarchy is narrated as the subject of drama: historical facts and events are dramatised. These are attempts to bring the royal house to life and to transfer historical

awareness/consciousness of the past from which the present can be reflected upon.

2) In other productions monarchic history serves as décor, the royal house is used in a decorative manner: a royal ride in a carriage with a waving queen (e.g., in a drama on the liberation of Holland in 1945), tea parties, like in *Soldaat van Oranje* [Soldier of Orange], again a World War II drama in which Queen Wilhelmina welcomes the hero of the story to her wartime accommodation in London. In this kind of production the Queen can hardly be considered a character. She only refers to herself as head of state, as a representative of the country, an icon.
3) In a few drama productions the royal house is also used as the subject of satire. In these cases, however, the story is situated in the present time and even in the future, not in history!

I shall elaborate mainly the first approach with the help of a few examples from the history of 'royal' television drama and touch only briefly on the satirical towards the end of this article. I have taken these examples from the production volume of the last thirty years (from 1969, the year in which the Broadcasting Act was legislated): all dramatisations of royal history. I have left out so-called reconstructions, based on archival footage and paper documents. As it turned out, the corpus is limited with only a few productions on the royal family having been made. These will be discussed below.

Monarchy and the women's movement

In the Netherlands a theatre tradition that addresses the life and times of monarchs is missing, unlike the UK, where one only needs to mention the kings in the plays of Shakespeare. In the 16th century royal people visiting a city or village were welcomed with so-called *tableaux vivants*. In the 17th century living pictures were more and more transformed into theatre plays, politically coloured, referring to royal history inside and outside the Netherlands. Despite these theatrical sources only a few plays in Dutch theatre history dealt with kings and queens. Recently two plays were performed, one (satirical) on the present royal family, named after the former girlfriend of crown prince Willem Alexander, Emily (in 1996). The other on former Queen Wilhelmina (performed in 1998) situated on the eve of World War II. The latter presents the Queen in rather a state of perplexity. She is torn between staying in her country with her people or leaving for London where the conditions for ruling the Netherlands in wartime seemed to be much better. In the end she leaves for London (as she really did at that time), a decision still regarded as controversial, as the public debates can tell.

Speaking about queens: a woman on the throne, might appear to be a very grateful subject for a beautiful 'human' piece of drama, especially when we keep in mind the fundamental questions that can be raised about the construction of dominant images. In 1990 a special series of commemorative postage stamps was distributed, portraying the four queens and celebrating a century of women on the throne in the Netherlands. In spite of the above-mentioned opportunities, only one dramatic television production was dedicated to a Dutch queen. Released in 1990, this documentary drama production *Emma, Koningin der Nederlanden* [Emma, Queen of the Netherlands] celebrated Emma's accession to the throne in 1890 from the perspective of the history and development of the women's movement. The setting, around 1900, offered an ideal arena. Also, a lot of British drama is set around 1900, a period in which several social changes took place: the emancipation of women, the rise of labour movements, etc., to mention the most important.

Emma is portrayed as a hard-working queen, above the political parties, giving love to the people, steering a middle course between loyalty to the Constitution and impartiality in discussions of the election bill, as a result of which, though, the Chamber was dissolved in 1894. Emma is subjected to the manipulations of ministers who do not tolerate a woman on the throne. Such a conflict may resound in current political affairs within certain ministerial departments, at least in the Netherlands. The gender perspective here connects historical fiction with the present time. This documentary drama pays a lot of attention to the relationship between the monarchy and the people, and to Emma's attempts to strengthen that relationship, laying the foundation for the 'serving monarchy' as we now know it.

As we can observe, this historical drama production joins representations that in the first place try to enhance a personal involvement in the monarchy among the audience. Besides it is exceptional in defining the essence and mentality of those days. Thus, it stresses universal elements relevant to our time and positions itself far from being costume drama. Moreover, the use of several narratives, the abandoning of realism for 'collage', may affect the popular understanding of history as construction, though relevant to the present. In this sense the production follows a modernist approach. It was broadcast by the NOS, a broadcasting organisation not rooted in pillarisation and without subscribers (membership), and as a consequence it takes up a marginal position, compared to the larger broadcasting companies with membership. It was founded to coordinate and realise everything that was suitable for combined efforts. Over the years it developed its own television drama policy and practice, especially emphasising content and form that are not quite so visible in other broadcasting companies. Its complementary character draws attention to the relationship between individuals and the social order, as in *Emma*, where the gender point of view brought to light some particular and hitherto unnoticed aspects regarding the position of queens and other high-ranking women.

Universal stories

At least in the Netherlands, it is mainly historical fiction that shows aloofness in developing a sense of contemporary history in terms of manners and customs. To elaborate further on this point we will now turn to the presentation of the symbol of symbols, *Willem van Oranje* [William of Orange], who lived from 1533-1584, 'stadtholder' in a republic at that time (only later they became kings), who inherited the principality of Orange and properties in the Netherlands (the north and the south, now Belgium). Throughout the ages the representation of Willem van Oranje has served to strengthen and intensify love for the House of Orange among the people, referring back to the most glorious moments in Orange history. For that purpose Willem van Oranje is quite a perfect subject. He has become the symbol of national unity, fighting for national freedom, for national independency (*id est* keeping the north and south together) and religious tolerance. Accordingly, these are the recurring themes in theatre plays, historical exhibitions, lectures, monuments, ceremonies and other remembrance activities, dedicated to William of Orange (Haitsma Mulier and Janssen 1984).

This is also true for the audio-visual productions, be it somewhat modified. The feature film from 1934 named after its main character (celebrating in fact Willem's birth 400 years ago) was used to support notions of national identity in times of crisis (the 1930s). The historical character was less important than the symbolic character, capable of unifying Dutch people around the Dutch flag for the benefit of a safe future.

In the eight-part television serial *Willem van Oranje* [William of Orange], broadcast in 1984, Willem's main symbolic function as a fighter for freedom (in thinking and believing) is foregrounded. Moreover the humanisation of the Father of Fatherland turns out to be the most important dramatic intention of this serial (in 1984 celebrating Willem's death 400 years earlier). Apart from notions of freedom and tolerance that are projected on to Willem van Oranje, he is reduced to human proportions, not as in British drama to 'superhumanise' the monarchy, but rather to revise the existing historical image of the Prince of Orange as a saint, as myth, into a man of flesh and blood.

Willem van Oranje is portrayed by star actor Jeroen Krabbé as a man who reacts emotionally and physically upon watching the execution of corporal punishments, which were quite normal at that time. In everyday life scenes he shows himself as a loving husband and father. For this purpose 20th century notions are set back in the 16th century (like those of a man with two feminist wives on his back, discussing his future marriage with his mistress) and as a result of that Willem van Oranje is an identifiable character, no super macho, but attractive as a man, showing his weaknesses without becoming a weak person. A boy, engaged in the welfare of his people, statesman rather than prince, political rather than royal. In the serial he dies as a human being, an advocate of freedom of belief and thinking, concerned about his people, who suffer from economic decline caused by the suppression of religious liberty.

It is a legitimate approach, which lacks however an historical understanding of the mentality and social relations of the 16th century that grounded the thinking and doing of the Prince and his contemporaries. Obviously writer and director intended less to comment on the time in which Willem lived, more on the Prince himself. Following traditional realistic conventions of story telling, the serial foregrounds the personal history of the Prince. It does not present history as construction, though it obviously develops a sense of history from a 1980s perspective. The result is a modern fairy tale, once there was a prince... defining history in general human terms. Universality beats historicisation.

The serial was broadcast by the AVRO, the eldest broadcasting company in the Netherlands, which from the beginning, claimed a position as a sort of 'national' broadcaster, unifying all possible pillars, opinions and beliefs present in Dutch society. Representing the so-called 'neutral' currents in Dutch society, it foregrounded synthesis and independence in its programming policy and more specifically the democratic principles of freedom and tolerance. National figure Willem van Oranje could easily help to bring to life AVRO's main ideological intentions and in the serial *Willem van Oranje* issues like freedom and tolerance are well elaborated and connected to the individual conflicts of a man, who, while appearing ordinary, carried heavy responsibilities.

The serial received severe criticism because of its shortcoming in not representing history in a contextually appropriate manner. It was, however, very popular with audiences and was also supported by the tabloid press who gave much attention to the serial and its main actors and actresses. An inquiry was even conducted among readers as to the best character performance. Most conspicuously, it was not Willem van Oranje who won, but his opposite number, the 'bad' character, Filip II, the Spanish king ruling the Netherlands.

In the discrepancy between the responses of audiences and historians, one can observe some false expectations among historians. The question is, however, to what measure historical fiction should write the history of mentality in terms of the political, social, and cultural questions of that time. The following example demonstrates how fiction can avoid this dilemma and still be capable of commenting on the past.

Thriller

In the most recent production on the monarchy (broadcast in winter 1998), the writer and director took the liberty of presenting an unusual version of monarchic history, exploring the relationship between fiction and reality, dramatising the question of historical truth. Following the conventional mode of the crime story, the makers demonstrate how truth and deception, fact and fiction are closely connected. It took them almost ten years to produce this eight-part serial, *Wij Alexander* [We Alexander] situated in 1909, the year of the birth of Queen Juliana.

The serial focusses on the third son of Willem III and Sophie, the excentric and schizophrenic Alexander who was said to have become crown prince after his two brothers died. Alexander died in 1884. He had some radically new ideas about the monarchy, like giving power to the people. In the serial, again situated in 1909, he lives, impersonated by patient number four in the psychiatric hospital where a young doctor, called Jan Giltay, who studied with Freud in Vienna, starts his career. This purely fictitious story (there was no Dr. Giltay in 1909 and there was no patient number four) serves as a framework for more or less authentic historical flashbacks, documenting parts of the life of Willem III and Sophie, and their three sons. The scriptwriter thus presents two fictional worlds, both situated in the past: 1909, and - about fifty years earlier - around 1850.

The serial is unconventional in its tendency to fly backwards and forwards between past and past. Dramaturgically it provides us with a 1909 perspective on the past, impersonated by the young Dr Giltay. He reflects the outsider's view that the audience can identify with, and leads the audience through this bizarre history, at the same time projecting its late 20th century knowledge on to the story. During the serial the young doctor becomes a tool in the hands of left-wing and right-wing people who want to use him to find out the truth about Alexander/patient number four: the right-wing people to protect the royal house and above all themselves, the left-wing people to prove that the royal house has died out with Alexander and Willem III. As the story develops the young doctor becomes more and more involved in the stories of patient number four, and together they finally escape from both the right- and left-wing people who in the end remain empty handed.

In the series everyone is looking for a certain box that contains documents damaging to the royal house. It is suggested in the serial that:

1) Willem III was impotent, suffering from syphilis, thanks to his dissolute life. Therefore he could never be the father of Wilhelmina, born as a result of his new marriage with Emma. Already in 1880 anarchists sneered at the birth of Wilhelmina, the newly born daughter of Emma and Willem III, as the red press tells us, and in the serial the same thing happens in 1909 when Juliana is born. And it is suggested that:
2) The court physician was responsible for Alexander's death, taking revenge on the royal house that dismissed him. The court physician is also looking for the box because the documents may be damaging to him as well. As the story develops the viewer finds out – together with the young Dr Giltay – that Alexander's lackey happened to be a witness to all this and that it was this lackey who administered the deadly medicine to Alexander, forced by the physician. The unbearable thought of having killed his beloved master made the lackey identify totally with Alexander and turned him into a patient. Only in the last part of the serial the mystery is revealed, and Alexander's lackey, finally freed from the burden, becomes himself again. The epilogue of the story shows how fifteen years later, the box is found and returned to the royal palace. The documents are burnt, carefully watched by the new queen, Wilhelmina!

The idea of a bastard royal house is interesting and controversial, especially in view of the function of the royal house in modern societies. In the serial the anarchistic cause, back in time, is presented as a reasonable one. Scriptwriter and director have focussed on the sensational story, rather than on the customs of those days. They tell an exciting story, embedded in the authentic signs of a time, a story about an institution that may be kept alive for the wrong reasons. The scriptwriter, also known in the Netherlands for writing detective novels, regularly bases his stories on authentic data. The life of Alexander, itself being a mix of secrecy and myth, offered him the necessary elements to create a crime story, a dramatic construction in which the writer could easily take up his own imaginitive position, stressing that he himself is responsible for the construction of history that is presented in the serial.

In this respect the serial does not particularly reflect the belief systems represented by the company that broadcast it, the KRO. Originally Catholic, KRO is formulating its identity in terms of offering a platform for different opinions within the Catholic community. It focusses mainly on human relationships in the community, a community that has to develop in line with social changes, adapting and changing Catholic standards and values to the new era. Unlike the other productions I discussed, an analysis of the serial *Wij Alexander* shows very little affinity with the general ideology of the broadcasting company involved, through which it legitimates its position in the Dutch broadcasting system. Here the conclusion is legitimate that writer and director took the space given to them by the company to develop their own story and that *vice versa* the KRO did not need a high profile Catholic serial at that moment in its history. Besides, KRO and writer and director worked together earlier on serials in the early 1990s and obviously the screenwriting and directing qualities were well respected and honoured with a follow-up.

Monarchy in popular consciousness: Concluding remarks

Most conspicuous in the audiovisual representation of the monarchy is the low profile, both quantitative and in terms of national identity. There have been scandals, like everywhere, but these have seldom been dramatised. As to the royal house, decency seems to be the rule and even the anarchistic attacks on the monarchy in *Wij Alexander* are not regarded as a dangerous threat to the position of the monarchy in the Netherlands, although it stimulated discussions on its symbolic function. Besides a few changes can be observed over time. The representation of the monarchy in the 1990s no longer needs a strictly realistic approach in which narrative closure guarantees unwelcome interpretations (as in the 1980s). Moreover, one can also argue that the concept of revealing the construction of the representation reflects a more critical and less accepted attitude towards the monarchy. On top of that, in the 1990s broadcasters in the Netherlands seem to be more reluctant in terms of articulating their traditional belief systems than in the 1980s, due to changing relations in the Dutch broadcasting system. Pluriformity as a concept is being kept alive though.

In terms of national identity, all productions tend to minimise the distance between monarch and people, though for different reasons and with different results. The representation of the monarchy is not associated with one particular nationally dominant moral or ideology. Here the pluriformity based Dutch broadcasting system still seems to do its work. Although in several productions human characteristics are prominent, they are always imbedded in political, historical and social contexts. Unlike the live television coverage of Queen's Day, historical fiction does not reinforce the royalist discourse, but modifies it by a revision of the 'family on the throne' concept.

A similar tendency can be observed in satirical productions on the monarchy, some of which caused scandals and led to discussions in Parliament, if only in the 1970s. Satirical productions have even made a parody of the ordinariness of the royal house, presenting Queen Juliana, peeling sprouts, and drinking sherry; presenting Queen Beatrix as an icon, stressing particularly her decorative function: drinking tea, cutting ribbons, being lonely and bored as, for example, in the feature film *Theo en Thea en de ontmaskeringvan het tenenkaasimperium* (impossible to translate, but for the record I suggest 'Theo and Thea and the unmasking of the toes cheese imperium', 1989). It has to be said that the satirical productions all were produced and broadcast by one broadcasting company, the VPRO, traditionally rooted in liberal Protestantism, that took up a progressive stance since the end of the 1960s. As a result of its deeply rooted interests in *avant-garde*, it experiments with new dramatic forms and explores the development of television language and contents.

In these fictional productions it is obvious that the monarchy is seen as a reflection of its function in society and is not presented as a strong and binding element in the nation. However, in the case of Willem van Oranje, he is probably seen to strongly represent virtues regarded to be typically Dutch, such as tolerance and freedom. In these productions he is also shown to embody the anti-authoritarian aspects of the present-day Dutch mentality. Notions of a common national past are obviously not projected on to the House of Orange.

Thus, unlike the issue of World War II, monarchic historical fiction does not reflect and express the idea of 'nation'; it does not produce dramatised 'coronations', so to speak, regarding the monarchy.

One of the explanations for these conclusions may be that a 'human' monarchy is already reconstructed in the popular consciousness, in the context of the anti-authoritarian attitude of the Dutch, and thus irrespective of the specific style of the reigning queen. Moreover, in the Netherlands, the function of the crown as a unifying force for the nation had little opportunity of developing because of its early republican experiences. Another more important explanation may be that the monarchy as *common history* is less rooted in popular consciousness than World War II. And for that reason one day a year, Queen's Day, may be enough. Historical fiction on the monarchy does not reflect the speaking position of the Netherlands in terms of royal discourse. As a weak aspect of common history, the monarchy provides room for a diverse collection of fictional stories that appeal to a diverse audience. Referring to David Morley (1995), I suggest that diverse stories about the royal past construct diverse identities in the present. In the case of historical fiction on the monarchy, pluriformity seems to be much more dominant than nationality, and in this sense it reveals and affirms an important cultural characteristic of Dutch society.

References

Anderson, Benedict 1983. *Imagined Communities: Reflections on the Origin and Spread of Nationalism*. London: Verso.

Burgoyne, Robert 1996. Modernism and the narrative of nation in JFK. Vivian Sobchak (ed.) 1996, *The Persistence of History: Cinema, Television and the Modern Event*. London: Routledge.

Dayan, Daniel & Elihu Katz 1995. Political Ceremony and Instant History. Anthony Smith (ed.), *Television: An international History*. Oxford: Oxford University Press.

Diependaal, Irene 1998. De familie op de troon: Het beeld van Oranje in populaire tijdschriften. *Tijdschrift voor Mediageschiedenis*, 1(2), 69-94.

Haitsma Mulier, Eco & Antoon Janssen 1984. *Willem van Oranje in de historie 1584-1984: Vier eeuwen beeldvorming en geschiedschrijving.* Utrecht: HES.

Hall, Stuart 1990. Cultural Identity and Diaspora. Jonathan Rutherford (ed.), *Identity. Community, Culture, Difference.* London: Lawrence and Wishart.

Hall, Stuart 1993. Cultural Identity in Question. S. Hall, D. Held & T. McGrew (eds.), *Modernity and its Futures.* Cambridge: Polity.

Jong, Ad de 1998. Dracht en eendracht: De politieke dimensie van klederdrachten, 1850-1920. D. Verhoeven (ed.), *Klederdracht en kleedgedrag: Het Kostuum Harer Majesteits onderdanen 1898-1998.* Nijmegen: SUN.

Leeuw, Sonja de 1999. Narrative and Identity. Case WWII. *Proceedings 1998 ISSEI Conference on Twentieth Century European Narratives: Tradition and Innovation.*

Morley, David 1995. No Place like Heimat. David Morley & Kevin Robins, (eds.), *Spaces of Identity.* London: Routledge.

Phillips, Louise 1999. Media discourse and the Danish monarchy: reconciling egalitarianism and royalism. *Media, Culture & Society* 21(2), 221-45.

Rosenstone, Robert 1995. *Revisioning History: Film and the Construction of a new Past.* Princeton: Princeton University Press.

Rutherford, Jonathan 1990. *Identity: Community, Culture, Difference.* London: Lawrence and Wishart.

Sobchak, Vivian (ed.) 1996. *The Persistence of History: Cinema, Television and the Modern Event.* London: Routledge.

Staiger, Janet 1996. Cinematic shots: the narration of violence. Vivian Sobchak (ed.), *The Persistence of History: Cinema, Television and the Modern Event*, London: Routledge.

Thijn, Ed van 1997. *Ons kostelijkste cultuurbezit: Over tolerantie, non-discriminatie en diversiteit.* Leiden: Leiden Universiteit.

Weeks, Jeffrey 1990. The Value of Difference. Jonathan Rutherford (ed.), *Identity. Community, Culture, Difference.* London: Lawrence and Wishart.

White, Hayden 1996. The modernist event. Vivian Sobchak (ed.), *The Persistence of History: Cinema, Television and the Modern Event.* London: Routledge.

About the Authors

Gunhild Agger

Gunhild Agger is Associate Professor in Communication at the Department of Communication, Aalborg University, Denmark. She has contributed to *Dansk Mediehistorie* (Danish Media History; Samleren, 1996-97) and to *Dansk Litteraturhistorie* (History of Danish Literature, 1983-85 (3rd ed. 2000)). She has published a number of articles on television drama, advertisements in a historical context, cultural theory and practice, and Russian and Danish literature. Her current research interests include television drama, theory of genre and style, history of the media, and cultural theory. Agger participated in the national research programme on 'The Aesthetics of Television' (1993-98), and has participated in the European research network on television drama 'Eurofiction' since 1998.

Christopher Anderson

Christopher Anderson is Associate Professor of Communication and Culture at Indiana University. A graduate of the University of Texas at Austin, he is the author of *Hollywood TV: The Studio System in the Fifties* (The University of Texas Press 1994). Anderson has been researching film and television history, theory, and criticism, as well as media industries and cultural production. He is now writing a history of the representation of crime on American television, and a monograph about the TV and film director, John Frankenheimer.

Niels Brügger

Niels Brügger is Associate Professor at the Department of Information and Media Studies, University of Aarhus, Denmark, and co-founder of The Centre for Internet Research. A graduate of the University of

Aarhus (Ph.D. 2000), he is the author of a number of articles and books on media, philosophy, culture, epistemology, and the internet, as well as being the co-editor of *Lyotard: Les Déplacements Philosophiques* (De Boeck-Wesmael 1993). His research interests are the history of media theory and the Internet. His ongoing research focuses on two aspects of the Internet: the Internet as a public sphere, and the website as text.

Michael Curtin

Michael Curtin is Associate Professor of Communication and Culture at Indiana University. A graduate of the University of Wisconsin (Ph.D. 1990), he is the author of *Redeeming the Wasteland: Television Documentary and Cold War Politics* (Rutgers, 1995) and co-editor of *Making and Selling Culture* (Wesleyan, 1996) and *The Revolution Wasn't Televised: Sixties Television and Social Conflict* (Routledge, 1997). Over the past four years, Curtin has been researching media industries in East Asia. His forthcoming book is entitled *Playing to the World's Biggest Audience: The Globalization of Chinese Film and TV*.

Per Jauert

Per Jauert is Associate Professor at the Department of Information and Media Studies, University of Aarhus, Denmark. A graduate of the University of Aarhus, he is the co-author of *Lokalradio og lokal-tv: Nu og i fremtiden* (Ministry of Culture, 1995). He has contributed to *Dansk Mediehistorie* (Danish Media History; Samleren, 1996-97), and he is the author of a number of articles on the medium of radio. His research interests include radio, media history, audio on the Internet, and audience research. His ongoing research focuses on the format development of radio after World War II.

Søren Kolstrup

Søren Kolstrup is Associate Professor at the Department of Information and Media Studies, University of Aarhus, Denmark. A graduate of the University of Aarhus he is the author of a number of articles on visual and written narration and narrative theory. His research interests are media history, visual semiotics and visual communication, especially computer-generated visual expression. His ongoing research focuses on the development of computer-mediated visual communication.

Sonja de Leeuw

Sonja de Leeuw is Associate Professor in Film and TV Studies at the Institute for Media and Representation, Utrecht University, the Netherlands. She is author of *Televisiedrama: Podium voor Identiteit. Een Onderzoek naar de Relatie Tussen Omroepidentiteit en Nederlands Televisiedrama 1969-1988* (Otto Cramwinckel, 1995). She has published a number of articles on television fiction, narrative and identity, and on documentary film and history. Her current research interests include television and the cultural construction of identity, the programming history of Dutch television fiction, and documentary film and video. She participates in the European research network on television drama 'Eurofiction' and in 'Questions of European Identity and the Eurovision Song Contest'. She is working on a recent history of Dutch television fiction.

Carin Åberg

Carin Åberg is Senior Research Fellow at the Department of Journalism, Media and Communication, Stockholm University and at the Department of Information Science, Media and Communication Unit, University of Uppsala, Sweden. A graduate of Stockholm University (Ph.D. 1999), she is the author of *The Sounds of Radio: On Radio as an Auditive Means of Communication* (Ph.D. thesis), *Den Omärkliga Tekniken: Radio och TV Produktion 1925-1985* (Natur & Kultur, 1999), and of a number of articles on radio analysis, radio listening, sense modality and perception. Åbergs research interests are communication theory, especially mediated communication. She is now engaged in a research project about sounds and images as means of communication (Swedish Council for Research in the Humanities and Social Sciences, HSFR).